The History of Latin Music

Stuart A. Kallen

LUCENT BOOKS
A part of Gale, Cengage Learning

GALE
CENGAGE Learning

Detroit • New York • San Francisco • New Haven, Conn • Waterville, Maine • London

LIBRARY OF CONGRESS CATALOGING-IN-PUBLICATION DATA

Kallen, Stuart A., 1955-
    The history of Latin music / by Stuart A. Kallen.
        pages cm. -- (The music library)
    Includes bibliographical references and index.
    ISBN 978-1-4205-0947-2 (hardcover)
    1. Music--Latin America--History and criticism--Juvenile literature. I. Title.
    ML3549.K35 2013
    781.64089'68--dc23
                                2012047681

Lucent Books
27500 Drake Rd
Farmington Hills MI 48331

ISBN-13: 978-1-4205-0947-2
ISBN-10: 1-4205-0947-0

Printed in the United States of America
1 2 3 4 5 6 7 17 16 15 14 13

CONTENTS

In the nineteenth century, English novelist Charles Kingsley wrote, "Music speaks straight to our hearts and spirits, to the very core and root of our souls. . . . Music soothes us, stirs us up . . . melts us to tears." As Kingsley stated, music is much more than just a pleasant arrangement of sounds. It is the resonance of emotion, a joyful noise, a human endeavor that can soothe the spirit or excite the soul. Musicians can also imitate the expressive palette of the earth, from the violent fury of a hurricane to the gentle flow of a babbling brook.

The word *music* is derived from the fabled Greek muses, the children of Apollo who ruled the realms of inspiration and imagination. Composers have long called upon the muses for help and insight. Music is not merely the result of emotions and pleasurable sensations, however.

Music is a discipline subject to formal study and analysis. It involves the juxtaposition of creative elements such as rhythm, melody, and harmony with intellectual aspects of composition, theory, and instrumentation. Like painters mixing red, blue, and yellow into thousands of colors, musicians blend these various elements to create classical symphonies, jazz improvisations, country ballads, and rock-and-roll tunes.

Throughout centuries of musical history, individual musical elements have been blended and modified in infinite ways. The resulting sounds may convey a whole range of moods, emotions, reactions, and messages. Music, then, is both an expression and reflection of human experience and emotion.

The foundations of modern musical styles were laid down by the first ancient musicians who used wood, rocks, animal skins—and their own bodies—to re-create the sounds of the natural world in which they lived. With their hands, their feet, and their very breath they ignited the passions of listeners and moved them to their feet. The dancing, in turn, had a mesmerizing and hypnotic effect that allowed people to transcend their worldly concerns. Through music they could achieve a level of shared experience that could not be found in other forms of communication. For this reason, music has always been part of religious endeavors, from ancient Egyptian spiritual ceremonies to modern Christian masses. And it has inspired dance movements from kings and queens spinning the minuet to punk rockers slamming together in a mosh pit.

By examining musical genres ranging from Western classical music to rock and roll, readers will find a new understanding of old music and develop an appreciation for new sounds. Books in Lucent's Music Library focus on the music, the musicians, the instruments, and on music's place in cultural history. The songs and artists examined may be easily found in the CD and sheet music collections of local libraries so that readers may study and enjoy the music covered in the books. Informative sidebars, annotated bibliographies, and complete indexes highlight the text in each volume and provide young readers with many opportunities for further discussion and research.

A Global Beat

The sounds of Latin America have had an enduring influence on many styles of music over the years. From the late nineteenth century to the modern age, the rhythmic beats of samba, rumba, mambo, tango, and salsa have played an important role in "Latinizing" the popular music heard around the world. Given the size and diversity of Latin America, it is not surprising that its music has been so influential.

The huge area that makes up Latin America contains about thirty countries and territories. It stretches from the southern border of the United States, through Central America and parts of the Caribbean, down to the tip of Chile, not far from Antarctica. Within it, nearly 600 million people speak several European languages and countless native dialects. Their music has drawn on a profusion of sounds, including indigenous harmonies and rhythms, African beats, Spanish song forms, European classical styles, and American rock and roll. These disparate elements, blended together over the course of centuries, have evolved into hundreds of musical styles. Yet each nation has its own distinctive and unique musical forms.

Cuban music, for example, contains equal portions of African and Spanish influence with few contributions from Amerindians. Peruvian music, by contrast, has strong

Amerindian roots blended with Spanish styles and only a dash of African rhythm. Some Mexican music draws inspiration from traditional Spanish ballads that are put to the German polka beat.

The Latin Tinge in Popular Music

Many Latin genres have had a major impact on popular music. The strongest Latin influences were felt in jazz music, which originated in New Orleans in the early twentieth century. The city, once ruled by the Spanish, had long been a center of trade for people from Mexico, Cuba, Puerto Rico, Venezuela, and Colombia. New Orleans was also home to black people whose ancestry stretched back to Africa, the Caribbean, and South America. In the 1910s, African American musicians such as Jelly Roll Morton adapted the rhythmic figures from Afro-Cuban bass and drum patterns to invent a new style of jazz called stride piano. This sound, which Morton called the "Latin tinge,"[1] formed the foundation of New Orleans jazz, a musical style that took the world

Two of the biggest contemporary acts in Latin music, Juanes and Juan Luis Guerra (left to right), perform together in New York City a few days after winning awards at the 2012 Latin Grammys.

Adopting Spanish Instruments

In 1615 Franciscan friar Juan de Torquemada described how the Aztec people adopted Spanish music and began making European instruments:

> The first instruments of music manufactured here were flutes, then oboes, and afterwards viols and bassoons and cornetts. After a while there was no single instrument used in churches which Indians in the larger towns had not learned to make and play. It became unnecessary to import any of these from Spain. One thing can be asserted without fear of contradiction; in all Christendom there is nowhere a greater abundance of flutes, sackbuts [early trombones], trumpets, and drums, than here in New Spain. Organs have also been installed here in nearly all the churches which are administered by the orders. However, with these, not the Indians but rather Spanish builders have taken charge of construction, since the Indians do not have capital for such larger enterprises. The Indians make the organs under supervision, and they play the organs in our monasteries and convents. The other instruments which serve for solace or delight on secular occasions are all made here by the Indians, who also play them: rebecs [three-string bowed instruments], guitars, trebles, viols, harps, spinets.

Quoted in Robert Stevenson. *Music in Aztec and Inca Territory.* Berkeley: University of California Press, 1968, p. 172.

by storm in the 1920s and has inspired countless musicians since that time.

The Latin tinge moved north to New York in the 1930s when Argentinean immigrants introduced tango music and dance to the American public. Tango musicians packed ballrooms and sold millions of records. The mambo and samba provoked similar fads in the 1940s and '50s. Even the hits of rock and roll, the most commercially successful music form in history, were heavily influenced by the Latin tinge, as music journalist Ed Morales writes:

Latin rhythms thoroughly permeated American pop— Afro-Cuban piano figures form the basis of the Isley Brothers' *Twist and Shout*, and the five-beat rhythm that pervades Buddy Holly's *Not Fade Away . . .* is essentially Afro-Cuban. . . . The Latin sound influenced the shaking and rattling behind rock and roll through New Orleans pianist/vocalist Fats Domino and the traces of habanera [Cuban dance music] found in the early stages of rockabilly. There were also musical influences from Mexico. The corrido tradition, based on Spanish ballads and important along the Texas-Mexico border, probably had an influence on . . . [Oklahoma folksinger] Woody Guthrie, Bob Dylan's forebear. The curious sound of the Farfisa organ, used as a novelty in late-1950s conjunto (Mexican-American dance) music, would become a signature of American psychedelic music half a decade later.[2]

While the Latin tinge influenced countless musicians, Latin performers have incorporated sounds of the north into their styles. Since the 1960s, Latin players have drawn inspiration not only from their traditional national sounds, but also from the Beatles, Bob Dylan, the blues of the Mississippi Delta, and the cool jazz from California. In the 2000s, newer sounds added to the spice of the Latin tinge, including European electronica dance music, Jamaican reggae, Afropop, and American hip-hop.

Strong Roots

By the 2010s, Latin American artists were among the top-selling acts in the world. The genre-bending Calle 13 from Puerto Rico won nineteen Latin Grammy Awards between 2006 and 2012 with a style that combined reggaeton, rock, and alternative rap. Colombian solo artist Juanes sold more than 15 million albums worldwide, blending the tropical sounds of bolero and merengue with jazz and classical elements. The Santo Domingan merengue singer Juan Luis

Guerra sold more than 30 million records and won numerous awards, including twelve Latin Grammys and two Billboard Music Awards.

Latin music has a history of constantly evolving and changing even while preserving elements of the past. Today, the story of Latin American music continues to progress. With its strong roots in Amerindian, African, European, and American cultures, the sounds emanating from Latin America are as diverse and multicultural as the modern world.

CHAPTER 1

Roots Music

M ore than five hundred years ago, people from all over the globe began flooding into the New World, a place now called Latin America. These people from Africa, Europe, and elsewhere imported their music, dances, and instruments. The sounds of the Spanish conquistadors, African slaves, and settlers from dozens of nations melded with those of the indigenous Americans. Over the centuries, this mingling of sound and culture created the roots of Latin music heard throughout the world today.

African elements included traditional rhythm patterns, instruments, and song structures that had been in use for thousands of years. The Europeans contributed a wide range of instruments along with specific poetic verse forms. People from Spain introduced music that was strongly influenced by traveling musicians from as far away as India, North Africa, and the Middle East. The indigenous people from Mexico to the Amazon rain forest added their own ancient forms that include vocal harmony styles and musical scales.

The Aztec Influence

The oldest musical traditions in Latin America are based on the sounds of the Maya, Aztec, and Inca societies that once dominated Central and South America. Archaeologists have unearthed ancient musical instruments made from bone, wood, ceramics, and other materials. These items have allowed scholars called ethnomusicologists to speculate about the ancient music of the Americas in its cultural context. Their work is aided by the indigenous peoples throughout the region, who continue to play music using instruments similar to those played in ancient times.

The Amerindians of Central and South America played three types of music: music for pleasure that inspired group singing and dance; functional music such as work songs and martial music; and the largest category, religious music used for rituals, magic, and communication with supernatural forces.

One of the major indigenous musical influences in Central America may be traced to the Aztec people who, according to Laurence E. Schmeckebier, lived in "well-planned cities with towering pyramids and impressive temples . . . and brilliantly colored palaces with extensive apartments and terraces." The Aztec culture also supported an "elaborate patronage of the arts such as poetry, the ritual dance, and music,"[3] according to Schmeckebier.

The Aztecs constructed a monetary system based on gold and copper coins. These were highly coveted by the Spanish

An illustration from the late sixteenth century depicts Aztec musicians playing a variety of instruments. The Aztec civilization is a major indigenous musical influence in Central America.

conquistadors, led by Hernán Cortés, who arrived in present-day Mexico in March of 1519. Within months, the conquistadors were at war with the Aztecs. In one early battle, the Aztecs captured several enemy fighters and sacrificed them on an altar set atop a tall pyramid. In 1568 Spanish soldier Bernal Díaz, a soldier in Cortés's army, described the music the Aztecs played during this bloody ceremony:

> As we were retreating we heard the sound of trumpets from the great [altar], which from its height dominates the whole City, and also a drum, a most dismal sound indeed it was, like an instrument of demons, as it resounded so that one could hear it two leagues [6 miles (9.6 kilometers)] off, and with it many small tambourines and shell trumpets, horns and whistles. . . . [And] the sound of them all was terrifying, and we all looked towards the lofty [altar] where they were being sounded, and saw that our comrades whom they had captured . . . were being carried by force up the steps, and they were taking them to be sacrificed. . . . [After] they had danced they immediately placed them on their backs . . . and with stone knives they sawed open their chests and drew out their palpitating hearts and offered them to the idols. . . . The Mexicans offered great sacrifice and celebrated festivals every night at their great [altar] at Tlatelolco and sounded their cursed drum, trumpets, kettle drums and shells, and uttered yells and howls.[4]

The songs were designed to terrorize the conquistadors and other enemies. As a result, for the next four centuries the music of indigenous Mexicans was dismissed by authors and music scholars as barbaric and frightful. The musicologists based their judgment not on written musical scores, which did not exist, but on the sounds that could be produced from the instruments commonly used by the Aztecs. In 1917 Alba Herrera y Ogazon, a member of the Mexican National Conservatory of Music, stated that these instruments were not "capable of producing either alone, or in conjunction with each other, a grateful harmony. . . . What these depraved sounds do conjure up are instead scenes of unrelieved ferocity."[5]

Herrera and other researchers did not recognize that the instruments of the Aztecs were capable of producing complex music. They crafted and played a wide variety of flutes made from clay, reeds, and animal and human bones. The conch shell was a particularly important instrument in war and was used to issue warning blasts. Several conch shells blown simultaneously by trumpeters could be heard up to 10 miles (16km) away in mountainous terrain.

Ceremonial instruments such as rattles were made from gourds or drilled bones filled with pebbles. The rhythm instrument known as a rasp consisted of grooved sur-

Inca Songs of Love and Loss

In 1613 Peru native Felipe Guáman Poma de Ayala wrote a 1,179-page book about Inca culture as it was at the time of the Spanish conquest in 1533. In this excerpt, Guáman Poma describes a type of indigenous love song called a haravi, whose themes would doubtlessly be familiar to fans of Latin music today:

When the haravi is sung . . . [the] pangs of love form their most frequent theme. The singer in a typical haravi complains that unlucky chance separates him from his beloved who is as beautiful as the yellow mountain flower of the Andes. . . . But though apart, he always thinks of her and pursues her like a precious but elusive reflection in the water. Her deceitful mother seeks to separate them. Her evil father also tries to keep them apart. But perhaps the Maker of All will one day take pity and reunite them. Even now when he thinks of her smiling eyes he loses his senses. He has been searching everywhere for her, traversing mountains, rivers, and villages. Now he can only sit and weep.

Quoted in Robert Stevenson. *The Music of Peru.* Washington, DC: Pan American Union, 1960, p. 141.

faces cut into bone, which a percussionist dragged a stick over. There were also several types of drums, including the *huéhuetl*, a horizontal drum on a three-legged stand played with the fingers, and the *teponaztli*, a drum played with drumsticks.

In the years following the Spanish conquest, the surviving Amerindians in the region set aside these native instruments and skillfully adopted the violins, trumpets, and organs brought to Mexico by the conquerors. These were often used to play songs taught to them by Christian missionaries. In secret, the Amerindians also used the European instruments to play their traditional music. In this manner, indigenous and Spanish music began to blend. This was the case not only with the Aztecs, but also with the indigenous Maya who lived in southern Mexico, Guatemala, Honduras, and elsewhere.

In the twenty-first century, the Maya continue to play the old songs, having adapted them to European instruments such as the trumpet and guitar. According to music scholar Richard Anderson:

> The music of the indigenous people of the southern Mexican state of Chiapas reflects many varied influences, past and present. . . . [All] share their basic Mayan roots with both Aztec and Spanish borrowings.[6]

Incan and Peruvian Music

Like the Aztecs in Mexico, the Inca who ruled present-day Bolivia, Ecuador, and Peru built a highly developed civilization with a strong musical legacy. Archaeologists have discovered a wide variety of flutes, drums, bone rasps, conch shells, and rattles throughout the region. According to musicologist Robert Stevenson, the "Andean peoples ruled by the Incas [perfected] the most advanced musical instruments known in either North or South America before Columbus's discovery."[7]

Flutes made from pelican, llama, puma, and deer bones were played alongside ocarinas, small clay wind instruments with three finger holes. The Incas also created trumpets from clay tubes as well as the skulls of dogs and deer.

Like many other instruments created by Amerindians, the trumpets were both musical instruments and works of art decorated with religious symbols. Stevenson describes a coiled clay trumpet, crafted to honor a cat god: "[A] feline juts out at one side of the [trumpet] bell. . . . Six stylized human heads rim the bell, their faces so turned that the three in each semicircle look towards the feline deity. Meanwhile his bulbous eyes peer above a mouthful of exposed teeth."[8]

In addition to flutes and trumpets, the Inca used many types of drums. These played extremely important roles in religious ceremonies, celebrations, wars, and long-distance communication. The largest drums were built from timber frames 9 to 11 feet (2.7 to 3.3m) across. The drumheads were made of leather and tied onto drum bodies with V-shaped straps.

Drummers could play distinct beats to convey messages to people as far as 9 miles (14km) away. The Incas also used the mammoth drums in celebrations performed only for the most elite members of society. The drums were mounted on the backs of several people and beaten by a woman while three hundred dancers linked arms. In a special ritual, the dancers took three steps forward and two steps back as they slowly approached the king. Although the huge drums are not used today, weddings, dances, and other festivities are celebrated with fifty-member bands that beat large, deep-toned drums called *bombos*.

Perhaps the most well-known Incan instrument to survive to modern times is the panpipe, or *antara*. This instrument features three to fifteen pipes of various lengths aligned in a row, each tube capable of producing a single note. Antaras were originally made from clay, but modern versions may be bamboo or wood. The pipes can be made of different lengths to allow musicians to play scales of five, six, or seven notes.

Using antaras, drums, and flutes, the Quechua people of Peru, Ecuador, and Bolivia continue to play their traditional songs. Many of the Amerindian musicians live in isolated regions of the Andes Mountains and produce music that is unique to each small village. The diverse music incor-

porates various scales, song structures, and playing styles, sometimes flavored with European sounds.

Traditional Andean music has spread far beyond South America. Peruvian folk bands have become ubiquitous in tourist towns and on college campuses in Europe, Canada, Japan, and North America. The folk musicians, dressed in ponchos and other traditional garb, play panpipes, bombos, guitars, *charangos* (a ten-string guitar), and notched-end flutes called *quenas*. One song that almost every one of these "poncho" bands plays is the eighteenth-century Peruvian folk anthem "El Cóndor Pasa." The piece was popularized in 1970 by the American pop duo Simon & Garfunkel, who recorded the song with Quechua musicians for the best-selling album *Bridge Over Troubled Water*.

Music of the Orinoco Delta

The native music of the Andean region has been changing and evolving since the Spanish arrived. However, there are parts of Mesoamerica so isolated that European and African styles have had little influence on the sounds of the indigenous people. Nonetheless, songs played by the Amerindian dwellers of the Amazon rain forest have inspired countless musicians in modern society. The music has been incorporated into modern rock, pop, and jazz songs. Short repetitive loops of the songs have also been digitally sampled and used in hip-hop and other styles of music.

The Warao, who live deep within the Amazon rain forest in Venezuela, have had only sporadic contact with outsiders. Their ancient musical traditions have remained unchanged for millennia. The twenty thousand or so Warao, whose name translates as "canoe people," live in houses built on stilts over isolated swampy islands in the Orinoco River delta. As is true among many indigenous cultures, music is central to the Warao way of life, and almost everybody sings as they work, play, and relax. Work songs, called *dakotutuma*, are sung for various tasks. Men sing special dakotutuma when they paddle canoes, which is often since canoes are the only form of transportation available to these river people.

Women have dakotutuma for gathering and cooking foods. Lullabies are particularly important, but these songs are meant to impart educational information to children, as ethnomusicologist Dale A. Olsen explains:

> Many of the Warao lullabies describe animals and spirits of the rain forest, most of them potentially dangerous. The majority of the animal lullabies are about jaguars: some refer to the physical characteristics of the jaguar, while others are about the jaguar's desire to eat babies. The song texts often tell the infant to go to sleep or it will be eaten by a supernatural jaguar (or some other infant-eating animal or spirit).[9]

Such lullabies serve to warn babies about the dangers found in the rain forest or describe poisonous plants that children should avoid. Others explain the types of work performed by adults, so that a child will expect to perform those tasks when he or she grows up. Research has shown that such lullabies also help infants learn to speak and understand their native language.

Supernatural Communication

The majority of Warao songs are categorized as theurgy, or supernatural communication. These songs often concern matters of birth, death, war, hunting, and healing. Joyous songs for fertility and harvesting are sung by all members of the tribe, while those written to address cosmic events are sung only by religious healers called shamans. The shamans specialize in curing spiritual and physical ailments through chanting, praying, and singing. The healing songs are used to communicate with good and evil spirits. These songs, said to be composed by the deities themselves, are passed down from one generation to the next or might be revealed to a shaman in a dream.

Shamans almost always accompany themselves with a special rattle, an instrument said to be a very powerful curing tool. These rattles have so much significance that shamans believe that they will die if the rattle is lost, stolen, or destroyed.

The Warao also use other, less important types of rattles for spiritual purposes. The *sewei* consists of small hooves, seeds, nuts, or even giant beetle wings strung together. This instrument, attached to a pole or worn around the ankle or wrist, makes a shaking sound during dance rituals. According to Warao belief, a vision of the first sewei came to a shaman during a dream. Since that time, only the most important people in the village are allowed to own one. Several other types of rattles are made from gourds mounted on sticks. These might be filled with rattling nuts or seeds, although the most spiritually significant rattles are filled with small quartz crystals and decorated parrot feathers, which are believed to hold magical powers.

Unlike many indigenous tribes, the Warao only have one type of drum, the *ehuru*, a double-headed drum in the shape of an hourglass, made from a hollow log. The drumhead is made from monkey or jaguar skin, and the drummer plays the instrument with a drumstick fashioned from a small tree branch.

Flutes made from deer bones and cane reeds are also common. The most sacred wind instrument among the Warao is the *isimoi*, an unusual instrument made from a long, tube-like reed threaded through an oblong gourd. The sound of the instrument is similar to the high-pitched whistles of birds in the forest. Comparable single-reed instruments are made by other indigenous people in the region, including the Waiwai, the Yekuana, and Goajiro.

The Warao also have several types of stringed instruments. During times of relaxation, singers may accompany themselves on a handmade violin called a *sekeseke* or on a four-stringed guitar-like instrument called a *wandora*.

African Drums

The musical culture of indigenous South Americans is similar to that found in Africa, where people have been incorporating music into work, play, and spiritual ceremonies for thousands of years. Like the Warao, Africans have songs for nearly every occasion. Not only do they sing educational lullabies to babies, but they have music for punishment as well. For example, the Akan of Ghana have special drums that are beaten as a petty thief is marched through the streets of a village.

Many ancient musical traditions traveled to Latin America with black slaves, who were first brought to Mesoamerica in the sixteenth century. The Africans came from at least 2,000 tribes that spoke more than 2,400 different languages. This diversity produced not only an incredible array of musical styles, but also a wide variety of traditional instruments that were adopted by musicians in nearly every part of Latin America.

Drums of African origin played an especially important role in the music of the New World. Drummers of the Yoruba and Ewe tribes in West Africa most often played a set, or core group, of two or three drums. These drums were later used by black Venezuelans in the coastal Barlovento region to play dance music known as the big drum dances, the round drum dances, and the small drum dances.

The three drums of African origin used for the round drum dances are called the *pujao*, *cruzado*, and *corridor*. They are all about 3 feet (1m) long and range from 18 to 26 inches (45 to 67cm) across, and are held between the thighs. One end of the drums is covered with goat, deer, or sloth skin, and they are played by drummers who use a traditional African playing style. One hand is used to strike the drumhead with a small stick. The heel of the other hand is pressed into the drumhead to change the tone in a dynamic manner.

Similar drums with African roots are found in the island nations of the Caribbean. The *gwo ka*, or big drum, is used in Guadeloupe. This drum has long been used to play seven traditional rhythms, each representing a different aspect of life. For example, the *toumblak* rhythm symbolizes love, fertility, and the earth. The *graj* rhythm signifies agricultural pursuits, while the *léwoz* is a warrior beat.

The *gwo ka* is similar to the *belé* drum of Martinique and the *belair* of Trinidad, which also have their roots in Africa. These are played in core groups of two and are traditionally used to accompany undertakings such as work, celebration, and dance.

Crosscutting Rhythms

In Cuba, Puerto Rico, and Jamaica, individual drummers are often accompanied by a second percussionist. This added player employs a set of small sticks, called *cata*, to beat out a counter-rhythm on the side of the big drum. According to ethnomusicologist John Storm Roberts, the term *cata* is likely derived from the Bantu-based languages spoken throughout Africa: "[Cata] is a verb root meaning 'to cut' . . . across or against something. . . . Indeed, cutting across the main rhythm is exactly the function of the *cata sticks*."[10]

What Roberts refers to as "cross-cutting rhythm" is also called polyrhythm. A drummer playing polyrhythm plays two separate independent beats at once. This gives music

Making a Bone Flute

When traveling, dancing, or gathering ceremonial herbs from the rain forest, the Warao people of Venezuela play flutes made from deer leg bones called tibias. Ethnomusicologist Dale A. Olsen describes how the flutes, named muhusemoi, are made:

> After he has selected the proper deer tibia, the maker opens both ends of the bone and removes as much marrow as he can with his knife. Then he places the bone in a place out of the reach of dogs but within the reach of cockroaches, which eat out the marrow within several days. After the bone is hollowed and dried, the maker forms the saddle-shaped mouthpiece with a knife. Then he . . . [uses] his fingers as rulers for finger-hole placement. Where the tip of his first finger falls he will drill the bottom finger hole with the sharpened point of a harpoon . . . a technique requiring only about one minute of effort per finger hole depending on the sharpness of the harpoon point. . . . The same techniques are used to determine the placement of the third finger hole and drill it out. Because Warao hands and Orinoco Delta deer tibias all differ in size, there is naturally a difference in the tone system of the final products.

Dale A. Olsen. *Music of the Warao of Venezuela.* Gainesville: University Press of Florida, 1996, pp. 78–79.

a constant rhythmic momentum and a strong, danceable beat. Polyrhythms, which are African in origin, are found in all styles of Latin music, as well as in rock, pop, jazz, and other genres.

Another ancient rhythm, called syncopation or backbeat, also has roots in Western Africa. The backbeat is a rhythm that accents the second and fourth beats of a four-beat measure. Like polyrhythms, backbeats form the rhythmic basis of Latin, rock, and pop music. Dale A. Olsen explains how these rhythms of African heritage differ from the beats of the indigenous Amerindians:

> Most Amerindian music featured a single, fairly steady, rhythmic pulse, with melodic syncopation in the vocal parts. A great deal of African music had complex, interlocking rhythms, played on [drums], or by slapping the body. . . . The rhythmic structures of African music have been greatly admired by people from many communities, and they have been widely adapted in some modified form to create new musical genres.[11]

Instruments with African Roots

Several stringed instruments from Africa are also found in Latin American roots music. The earth bow, found in Haiti and the Dominican Republic, combines a drum with a bow and musical string made from tightly rolled animal intestine. True to its name, the earth bow consists of a bow planted in the earth. A bent sapling with a string, similar to a hunting bow, is placed on a drumhead covering a hole in the ground. The string is hit with a short stick while the player bends the bow to change the note produced by the string.

A more portable instrument was produced with a bow attached to a gourd that worked as a resonator, amplifying the sound of the string when it is hit. A different version of this instrument consisted of a stick attached to a gourd with several horsehair strings that were strummed. These instruments were precursors to the modern banjo. Although the banjo is associated with American bluegrass music today, during the 1700s, black and Hispanic musicians throughout the Caribbean played the instrument. Depending on

The belé drum of Martinique is one of the traditional instruments in the Americas with African roots.

the island, the banjo was variously called the *bangil*, *banzar*, *bangie*, and *banjah*.

A more traditional Latin instrument, the thumb piano or mbira, also originated in Africa. In its original form, the mbira was a board with bamboo prongs fastened to it. Each prong produced a different note when plucked with the thumb. In the nineteenth century, people began making mbiras from the metal prongs attached to cigar boxes or packing crates. Whatever its form, the mbira is called the *marimbula* or *marimbola* in Spanish-speaking countries such as Cuba and Puerto Rico. In French-speaking Trinidad, it is the *basse-en-boîte*, or bass box. In English-speaking Jamaica, the mbira is referred to as the rumba box. Popular for centuries, the mbira provides both musical and rhythmic accompaniment to Caribbean dance music.

The Afro-Spanish Connection

In addition to importing a wide range of musical instruments to the New World, Africans brought singing techniques that profoundly impacted Latin music, as well as rock and other styles. One of the singing styles, known as call-and-response, combines rhythm and melody and encourages community participation.

The call-and-response technique revolves around a song leader singing a line and a group of singers repeating it. Oftentimes the singer will improvise, or make up, the first phrase while the chorus sings the same response after each phrase. This type of interaction brings together two significant features of African music: improvisation and repetition. While the repetition provides a driving, rhythmic force, the improvised words and musical phrases give the song an entertaining impulsiveness. As John Storm Roberts explains:

> [The] human voice is . . . of overriding importance; call-and-response singing is by far the most common form of group vocal technique. African music is often built up by the use of relatively short musical phrases, often repeated or of longer lines made up of phrases never repeated in just the same form. Rhythm and,

A Mexican woman in a traditional Aztec costume plays a banjo in the town of Tequisquiapan, Mexico. The modern banjo has its roots in African stringed instruments.

more generally, a percussive approach are fundamental. And above all, music is a communal functional expression to a far greater degree than in most other parts of the world.[12]

When the storied African rhythmic and communal song traditions reached the New World, they had themselves been transformed by wandering traders. Their connection to Latin America occurred through a series of historical events that began in the early eighth century on the Iberian peninsula, the location of present-day Spain and Portugal.

Between 711 and 1492, the Moors from Morocco in North Africa ruled Iberia, which was a center of world commerce and culture during that time. The traveling merchants who conducted business were Roman Christians, Palestinian Jews, North African Arabs, African blacks, and Eastern European Gypsies. When people socialized, they traded musical instruments and singing styles from their native regions. Musicians from the Middle East brought flutes and early versions of violins as well as the *laúd*, a stringed instrument that was later transformed into the lute and guitar. Africans brought their own stringed instruments and a wide variety of drums, rattles, and other rhythm instruments.

During the Moorish era, traditional songs were traded as eagerly as instruments. Middle Easterners contributed a vocal style based on the vocal trill, or rapid tremolo. This method of creating wavering notes was adapted by nomadic Gypsies who sang nostalgically of homelessness and loss. Troubadours from France contributed wistful love songs about unattainable women. The Spanish incorporated the troubadour form into a song style called *décima* that is based on a lyrical pattern featuring ten lines of eight syllables each.

Décima was carried to the Canary Islands off the coast of Africa by Spanish sailors and traders. There it was adopted by the mixed-race population composed of Africans and Spaniards. The décima song pattern was particularly interesting to African drummers because of the repetitive rhythm of the lyrics. Décima was carried by the Spanish to the New World, and by the early twentieth century it had influenced a wide variety of Latin styles. According to Ed Morales: "The décima form survives today in the modern Latin ballad, known as bolero, the Mexican corrido, the Colombian vallenato, the Puerto Rican décima or seis, the Cuban trova, and even the folk songs of Argentine nueva cancion."[13]

Conceived and reworked over the centuries by people from five continents, décima is the perfect symbol for Latin music. The sounds bring together the rhythms of indigenous people, the melodies of wandering traders, and the words of pensive poets. Regardless of where Latin music is played—whether in northern Mexico, the Caribbean islands, or in the southernmost reaches of Chile—its unique melodies and instruments once played important roles in ancient societies, from African tribes to the Incas and Aztecs. The sounds continue to circle the globe in the twenty-first century.

CHAPTER 2

Caribbean Spice

In 1492 when Christopher Columbus sailed from Spain to the Caribbean islands with sailors of European, African, and Middle Eastern descent, he unknowingly set in motion a mixing of world musical cultures that continues to this day. In the centuries that followed, a multiracial mix of people flooded into the Caribbean from Spain, France, England, and African nations such as the Canary Islands, Egypt, Ghana, Nigeria, Senegal, and Benin. Each group brought its own musical traditions. As time passed, the styles were mixed, blended, and expanded into the red-hot sounds of modern Latin-Caribbean music.

Cuban Musical Culture

In the early sixteenth century, when Spanish colonizers began to arrive in the New World in large numbers, the Taino occupied the island of Cuba. At that time, the primary percussion instruments of the Taino and the other original inhabitants of the Caribbean, the Carib Indians, were maracas and guiros. Maracas are rattles traditionally made from small gourds filled with pebbles or seeds and mounted on sticks. The guiro is a larger gourd with parallel notches cut into it. Often called a scraper, the instrument is played by a percussionist scraping a wooden stick over the notches to produce a danceable ratchet-like sound.

The Spanish annihilated the native population by 1550, but guiros and maracas found a place in the music played by the new arrivals. In the following years, Spanish settlers brought the guitar, the twelve-string laúd, and the three-string *bandurria* to Cuba along with a variety of woodwinds, brass horns, and drums. The Spanish also imported thousands of African slaves from the nations of Benin, Nigeria, Congo, and Cameroon. These people, many of Yoruba descent, brought their own musical traditions based on group drumming, singing, and dancing. By the time slavery was abolished in Cuba in 1886, more than a million people of African descent were living on the island.

The mix of European and African cultures in the booming New World colonies created a musical stew composed of many ingredients. The Creole settlers (Caribbean-born people of Spanish descent) particularly enjoyed military bands that featured trumpets, clarinets, fifes, and drums. Martial bands played at all official ceremonies and during celebrations. Church music was also important in Cuba, and hymns based on religious texts were sung on Sundays and religious holidays. Musicians accompanied church choirs by playing organs, bassoons, flutes, oboes, viols, and violins. The musicians in both church orchestras and military bands were often black or of mixed race.

Secular music also blossomed in Cuba. By the early nineteenth century, there were at least fifty public dance halls in Havana, the capital city. Since the musicians who played the dance halls were paid poorly or not at all, few Creoles played in Cuban dance bands. Instead, the work was performed by slaves and free blacks. In 1800 musician Antonio Valle Hernández commented on this phenomenon: "The arts which, in other countries, are the occupation of respected, well-born white people, here are the near-monopoly of people of color."[14]

As often happens with poorly paid musicians, Cuba's performers learned to play all styles of music to improve their

Preserving African Traditions

It is estimated that more than six hundred thousand Africans were brought to Cuba to work as slaves between the mid-1600s and 1886 when slavery was finally abolished on the island. The Spanish divided slaves into groups called *cabildos* according to their region, town, or tribal origins. The *cabildos* served as mutual aid societies that taught newcomers how to live within Cuba's slave system. Although the Spanish founded the *cabildos* to defuse tensions between Africans and slave masters, the organizations grew into cultural institutions that enabled slaves to preserve their traditional music, songs, dances, and religious beliefs.

Each cabildo was organized into a social hierarchy under which members elected a king or queen to lead the group. The cabildos, with names like the Cabildo of the Royal Congos, met in temples where magical objects devoted to the gods, or orishas, were displayed. Members of the cabildos played drums and danced while wearing costumes and masks. On Spanish religious holidays, such as Epiphany or Corpus Christi, the slaves were allowed to perform in the streets. Although the cabildos were meant to divide the slaves into separate ethnic groups, people intermingled in urban areas. Through this blending of cultures, new and unique music emerged.

chances of finding work. According to Latin music scholar Maya Roy:

> For most of the musicians of color, the boundaries between classical, religious, and popular music were blurred, since they were proficient in all three types. With their instrumental expertise and their [African] musical heritage, musicians of color created original scores with a typical Creole flavor that won over the popular public, and then fashionable high society as well.[15]

Music of the Gods

Even as black musicians were gaining acceptance for their Creolized music, many also maintained their Yoruban traditions. Although the Spanish baptized all slaves into Roman Catholicism, they also allowed them to practice their traditional religions, which were centered on drumming and dancing. Much as they had done with music, the black population blended traditional African and Spanish religious practices. This melding of spiritual beliefs produced a religion called Santeria, whose practitioners worshiped deities, or orisha, which combined characteristics of Yoruban gods with those of Catholic saints.

Dispensing with church organs and choirs, Santeria worship was centered around a two-headed drum called a *batá*. Then as now, these drums were played in threes, with sets consisting of a large, medium, and small drum. The rim of the largest, lowest-pitched drum, the *iyá*, is fitted with small brass bells that enhance the drum's sound. The medium batá is called the *itótele*, and the smallest, highest-pitched drum is called an *okónkolo*. Since each drum can produce

Drummers participate in a Santeria ceremony in Havana, Cuba, in 2011. The batá drum is an integral part of the religious practice.

two tones from its double heads, a set of batá can emit six tones. Each of these tones may be modified by the intensity of the drummer's hand slap and the area where the drumhead is hit.

A complex array of drum tones is important to Santeria worship because practitioners believe each orisha can be called down to earth only with a unique musical rhythm called a toque. Ceremonies open with the lead drummer playing a toque on the iyá for a specific orisha. The itótele player plays a counterpoint to the iyá, and the okónkolo begins a steady rhythm pattern. Maya Roy describes the importance of this ritual:

> Sacred and consecrated instruments . . . these drums speak; they are the voice that calls the deities, and the divinities speak through the drums. Initially, the combination of rhythmic patterns, melodic inflections, and timbres reproduced the tonal sequences of the Yoruba language. There is a special musical language of the drums that corresponds to each divinity, as well as special songs and dances. . . . The *olubatá* [drummers] who play the sacred drums—the only ones authorized to ritually consecrate them—have passed down, over the centuries, an extremely complex body of knowledge: a multitude of melodic/rhythmic patterns, as well as the skill of making the transition from one rhythmic pattern to another in a conversation with the same divinity or in going from one invocation to another.[16]

By the middle of the twentieth century, the musical and religious traditions of Santeria had spread beyond Cuba to Puerto Rico, and into the United States, especially New York City and Miami. Santeria chants, sung in the Yoruba language, have been recorded by Latin music stars including Celia Cruz and Mongo Santamaria, and even white rockers such as David Byrne, the founder of the group Talking Heads.

"Let's Get Going"

In Cuba, the Santeria rhythms were also played in a secularized form called rumba. Unlike the ritual music of Santeria,

Packing Crate Percussion

Rumba rhythms originated in the working-class black communities in Havana, Cuba, in the 1890s. As Latin music scholar Maya Roy writes, rumba players were able to fashion remarkable percussion instruments from the packing crates they found in their workplaces:

> The first . . . percussion instruments were large wooden crates of varying shapes, known by the generic name of *cajón*. The musicians generally preferred the crates used for shipping codfish and, for the smallest instruments, the crates for packing candles. The wooden parts would be cut out and polished to improve their resonance; then they were rejoined with nails or glue. Later, *cajóns* were made for a specifically musical usage [in sets of three]. . . . The stable rhythmic pattern is established by the *tumbador* (or *salidor*), the largest of the *cajóns*, which the musician plays seated. The instrument is beaten according to different styles (including with a closed fist) on the sides or on one side and on the front, with one hand playing in counterpoint to the other. The small *cajón*, also called *repicador*, is used for improvising. The musician holds it in place by squeezing it between the knees. The last *cajón*, of a middle register, is called *tresdos*; it is linked rhythmically to the *tumbador*.

Maya Roy. *Cuban Music*. Princeton, NJ: Markus Wiener Publishers, 2002, p. 51.

in which specific beats are played on low-pitched drums, the rumba beat is improvised on high-pitched percussion instruments.

Rumba was originally played on the streets and at parties by tradesmen working in Havana. The name of this exciting and passionate music literally means "form a path," or in street slang, "let's get going." Rumba originated among

Cuba's poorest citizens—workers who used whatever tools were at hand to play rumba rhythms. Farmworkers set a beat with hoes and shovels; dockworkers whacked packing crates, or *cajóns*, with tools. Bakers beat out the rumba rhythms on flour crates with their fists and cooking utensils. The rumba performance is described by author and filmmaker Isabelle Leymarie as "a complex and gripping ritual including drumming, singing, declamation [dramatic speech] and dancing [that] thrives in back alleys and courtyards, where African blood courses strongly in the veins of the inhabitants."[17]

During the twentieth century, packing crates were replaced with drums and shakers of all shapes and sizes. Hardwood blocks, known as claves, also became central to rumba rhythm. These long dowels were originally used as pegs to join boards in shipbuilding. Claves are struck in patterns of either two beats followed by three beats or the reverse, three beats followed by two. This sets a steady and unchanging rhythm pattern to keep the improvisations of the drummers on beat while giving the music an expressive charge. Cuban music historian Fernando Ortiz explains the significance of the clave:

> Aside from its rhythmic importance in musical practice, the Cuban clave is itself, by virtue of its simplicity and striking timbre, a melodic exclamation filled with emotion. . . . There is something about [the clave] that eludes the typical opaque sound of wood. . . . Its vibrations create an almost crystalline or metallic resonance.[18]

Cuban rumba players set the beat with intricate polyrhythms. A lead singer, called *El Gallo*, or the Rooster, crows improvised lyrics above the cacophonous cadence of the percussion. Lyrics are patterned in stanzas of four lines called quatrains or in eight-syllable, ten-line verses based on Spanish *décima* song patterns. The lyrics often incorporated news from the streets, political satire, and commentary about current events. Group participation was originally key to the rumba and used the traditional African call-and-response technique.

The insistently rhythmic music of rumba inspired its own dance, also called rumba. There are three styles of rumba dance. The *yambú* can be slow and hypnotic, while the *guaguancó* is a fast dance featuring couples who perform provocative moves such as pelvic thrusting. The *columbia*, also a fast dance, is only performed by men, who often aggressively joust and parry in mock knife fights.

The Rise of *Son*

As rumba was developing in Cuba's urban areas, another form of percussion-only music, called *son*, evolved in the mountainous Oriente Province in eastern Cuba. The first *son* musicians were rural workers who combined syncopated African rhythms with melody lines that were independent of the percussive beat. *Son* has several similarities to rumba: The music follows a constant beat set down by a clave player, and it has a ten-line *décima* lyric pattern.

In the late 1800s, Nené Manfugás brought the sounds of *son montuno*, or son of the mountains, to Santiago in east Cuba. Manfugás played a guitar-like instrument called a *tres*, which has three double strings. *Son* bands added bongos, maracas, guitars, and singers to perform the fast-paced rhythmic music. By the 1910s, the *son* sound had spread to Havana, carried by migrating agricultural workers and day laborers. As music that originated among the poor, *son* was at first condemned as decadent by the government and upper-class citizens of the capital. However, *son* continued to flourish. By the end of the 1920s, many *son* orchestras had grown to include six or seven players, including trumpeters and bassists. The joyful sounds emanating from these sextets and septets proved to be irresistible to Havana's most affluent citizens, and *son* emerged as the national sound of the Cuban people.

The red-hot dance group Sexteto Habanero, featuring a pair of lead vocalists and a sizzling trumpet, was the first to achieve widespread popularity in Havana. The group's records were sold in the United States and Europe, and *son* quickly achieved international popularity. Hollywood soon picked up on the trend. In the 1930s, the movie *Cuban Love Song* featured the orchestra led by famed Cuban pianist and composer Ernesto Lecuona, while the film *Rumba*, with

Compay Segundo and Ry Cooder (left to right) of Buena Vista Social Club perform in 1998. Their self-titled album and documentary brought Cuban son *music to a worldwide audience.*

bandleader Xavier Cugat, introduced Cuban *son* music to countless Americans.

The *son* fad ended abruptly in 1959 when communist dictator Fidel Castro took control of Cuba, prompting the U.S. government to institute an embargo against the nation. As their record sales and international gigs dried up, Cuba's most talented *son* musicians were suddenly unemployed. Many eventually died or disappeared. In 1995, however, a few remaining *son* musicians, many of them past eighty years of age, were contacted by slide guitar player and Los Angeles native Ry Cooder, who had traveled to Cuba to learn about the musical style.

When Cooder played with the old musicians, he was amazed to find that they had retained their musical skills despite long years of working menial jobs. Cooder contacted arranger Juan de Marcos González to make a record with the veterans. In 1996 the album *Buena Vista Social Club* was released to widespread acclaim. The record featured master vocalists Ibrahim Ferrer, Omara Portuondo, and Pio Leyva; Afro-Cuban pianist Rubén González; bassist

Orlando "Cachaito" López; tres player Eliades Ochoa; and trumpeter Manuel "Guajiro" Mirabal.

Buena Vista Social Club eventually sold more than 2 million copies, and demand for the group was so great that a tour of Europe and the United States followed, ending at the famed Carnegie Hall in New York. The album won several Grammys, and in 1999, Wim Wenders released a film of the same name, which documents the recording of the album and parts of the concert tour. The popular record and film set off a Cuban music explosion in the late 1990s, and the *son* style once again was embraced by listeners across the globe.

The Afro-Cuban Spice Hits New York

The music featured in *Buena Vista Social Club* recalled a time when other forms of Cuban music, in addition to *son*, were wildly popular in the United States. These styles caught the public's attention after World War II, when New York was a prime destination for Cuban performers who combined Latin rhythms and melodies with big band jazz and swing. The resulting style, called Afro-Cuban jazz, was popularized by Cuban musicians such as Mario Bauzá and Frank Raul Grillo, also known as Machito. Their sound attracted African American jazz musicians, including trumpeter Dizzy Gillespie, who helped popularize the music among a wider audience. As Gillespie states:

> I really became interested in bringing Latin and especially Afro-Cuban influences into my music. . . . No one was playing that type of music. . . . No one was doing that. I became very fascinated with the possibilities for expanding and enriching jazz rhythmically and phonically through the use of Afro-Cuban rhythmic and melodic devices.[19]

As Gillespie was incorporating the Latin sounds into American jazz, a new dance rhythm in Havana called the cha-cha-cha made its way to New York. This conga-driven sound soon acquired the name mambo, and New York dancers rapidly fell into the fevered grip of "mambo mania."

The epicenter of this fad, the Palladium Ballroom in midtown Manhattan, was often packed with movie stars, jazz musicians, sports figures, and a multicultural mix of African Americans, Hispanics, and European Americans. Dancers competed to attract the most attention with ferocious acrobatics, moving to the sounds of the Mambo Aces, Tito Rodriguez, Machito's Afro-Cuban Orchestra, and others.

Tito Puente, known as the King of Mambo, or *El Rey*, was one of the most popular acts. Puente was a percussionist, arranger, and bandleader who eventually recorded more than one hundred albums, published more than four hundred compositions, and won four Grammy awards. He was credited with introducing the timbales—double tom-tom drums played with sticks—to the Afro-Cuban sound. He also played the trap drums, the conga drums, the claves, the piano, and occasionally, the saxophone and clarinet.

Cuban dance team Pete and Millie demonstrate the mambo at New York City's Palladium Ballroom in 1954.

"Spice It Up a Little"

When the Palladium closed in the mid-1960s, the Afro-Cuban fad had run its course. By this time, millions of immigrants from Puerto Rico were living in New York, and a new sound was developing in the Puerto Rican neighborhood known as El Barrio. This sound, called salsa, incorporated Cuban *son*, Puerto Rican *plena*, Dominican merengue, mambo, rumba, and American rock and roll, soul, and funk.

The term *salsa*, or sauce, was first used in a musical context by renowned Cuban composer and singer Ignacio Piñeiro, who wrote the hit *son* song "Enchale Salsita" in 1937. The song's title means "spice it up a little." Piñeiro wrote the song referring not to music, but to the bland American food that he was served while on tour in the United States. Nonetheless, soon after the song was released, dancers in New York nightclubs began using the term to urge bands to add some hot Latin spice to their music. By the mid-1970s, there was plenty of spice in the salsa music of New York. Bands played the driving, danceable musical style in groups featuring the clave, piano, bass, guitar, trumpet, conga, timbale, bongo, and cowbell.

With its broad mix of musical forms, the salsa genre is difficult to describe. However, as New York sociologist Vernon W. Boggs explains, the music is informed by the poverty and hopelessness many Puerto Rican immigrants face in the United States:

> [Salsa] represents a new phase in the evolution of Afro-Hispanic culture: that of the urban-industrial working class. . . . The best salsa songs voice the problems of this disadvantaged class. Scarcity, violence, inequality, marginality, and desperation are translated into the words and music of the popular singers and performers from the barrio. Street fights and love affairs marked by treason and suspicion have replaced the romantic themes of [traditional Puerto Rican music]. The world of *salsa* is full of allusions to the factory, the supermarket, welfare programs, or urban decay. . . . Musically, *salsa* is as far removed from the cha-cha-cha as is the trombone from the violin: the carefully arranged sound of the latter has yielded to the violent

orchestration of the former. The pace of life has quickened, and so has the rhythm of the music.[20]

The tough life of the Latino barrio was a strong influence on one of the founding fathers of the salsa movement, trombonist Willie Colón. Born in the heart of the Latino Bronx in 1950, Colón learned the lyrics to traditional Puerto Rican folk songs from his grandmother as she rocked him to sleep every night. After Colón signed with New York's Fania record label at the age of seventeen, his first album, *El Malo*, sold three hundred thousand copies. With this unprecedented success behind him, Colón continued to innovate. In the late 1960s, he was among the first to use the trombone as a lead instrument. Colón also wrote music that placed less emphasis on the traditional clave beat while incorporating dance rhythms from Colombia, Panama, Brazil, Cuba, and Puerto Rico.

Colón went on to collaborate with musical giants such as the Fania All Stars, Héctor Lavoe, and Celia Cruz, a singer known as the Queen of Salsa. In 1978 Colón worked with Panamanian poet, singer, and movie star Rubén Blades. Their album of socially conscious songs, *Siembra*, was the best-selling salsa album of the era.

Salsa Romantica

During the 1980s, salsa lyrics with overt political content fell out of style and were replaced by a new form called *salsa romantica*, or romantic salsa. This music features handsome singers with soft, smooth delivery who croon sentimental lyrics about love at a slow, sensuous tempo. In 1988 singer Lalo Rodríguez defined the style with the international hit "Ven, Devórame Otra Vez" ("Come, Devour Me Again"). According to Ed Morales, the song "establishes the basic narrative strategy of the salsa romantica [singer]: I am incapable of resisting a beautiful woman, and I hope that she will give herself to me, because otherwise I might die right here and now."[21] The sentiments expressed by Rodríguez proved to be irresistible to the record-buying public, and salsa romantica singers have sold millions of records internationally.

Gloria Estefan, seen here performing in 1998, reintroduced Latin music to pop audiences in the United States and paved the way for a new wave of crossover Latin artists.

As the status of salsa continued to grow, the center of Latin music production shifted from New York to Miami. The southern salsa influence was nowhere more obvious than in the music of Gloria Estefan's Miami Sound Machine. Estefan, born in Cuba, grew up in Miami in the 1960s and formed the Miami Sound Machine with her husband, Emilio, in 1979. By the mid-1980s, the group was one of the top bands in the United States, playing a mix of Latin salsa rhythms, disco, soul, and rock.

Estefan, who began a solo career in 1990, was responsible for introducing Latin music styles to pop audiences. Her success spawned a new wave of extremely successful Latin crossover artists. One of these artists, Marc Anthony, born Marco Antonio Muniz in New York's Barrio, grew up listening to American soul music as well as Rubén Blades and Willie Colón. Anthony's big break came when he was hired as a backup singer for the teen pop sensation Backstreet Boys. In 1991 Anthony decided to return to his salsa roots, left the Backstreet Boys, and began recording salsa in Spanish. By 2000, after recording four albums in Spanish and two in English, Anthony was one of the top international stars of Latin music. He continues to make music in the 2010s.

Infectious Merengue Beats

As the popularity of salsa exploded, another Latin-Caribbean sound began attracting devotees to smaller clubs

A güira player performs with a band in Santo Domingo, Dominican Republic, in 1946. The güira dates back to the Carib people, the original inhabitants of islands in the Caribbean.

in New York. The music and dance style called merengue originally evolved in the Dominican Republic among the rural people of Congo African heritage. In the early twentieth century, merengue was played by bands featuring an accordion, stand-up bass, *tambora* drum, and the güira, a unique percussion instrument. The güira is made from a piece of metal cut from a 5-gallon (19-liter) gas can, which is perforated with dozens of holes. The instrument is played with a stiff brush, which provides a distinct rasping sound.

Merengue musicians play a loping, infectious dance beat at a breakneck tempo. In the 1930s, merengue became the national music and dance style of the Dominican Republic after it was promoted by the nation's dictator Rafael Trujillo. In the 1970s, the sound was transported to New York by Dominican immigrants who settled in Washington Heights. When the salsa craze hit New York, merengue bands often shared the concert-hall stage with salsa bands.

In the 1980s, the merengue sound was modernized by Wilfrido "El Barbarazo" Vargas, who added rock, soul, jazz, reggae, and Brazilian samba songs to the musical mix. Playing other song genres with merengue rhythms is known as *fusilamiento*, or shooting. Fusilamiento helped push the style's popularity to new heights, and sales of merengue songs even beat out those of salsa records in some places. In the twenty-first century, merengue has been fused with hip-hop, techno, electronic sampling, and other modern techniques to create a new, ultrafast fusilamiento style.

Reggaeton "Riddims"

Reggaeton, which merges hip-hop and other styles into a completely unique sound, is another island-born genre with a long musical history. In the early 1900s, when the United States government was building the Panama Canal, thousands of English-speaking Jamaicans moved to Panama to work on the massive engineering project. Many of these migrant workers learned Spanish. When the canal was finished, some Jamaicans stayed in Panama, while others moved on to seek work in Puerto Rico.

Daddy Yankee: Reggaeton Royalty

Reggaeton music was a well-established and popular style in Puerto Rico in the early 2000s, but few outside the island had ever heard beat-based Latin hip-hop music. In 2004 Daddy Yankee changed all that with his party-oriented international reggaeton hit "Gasolina." The song was the lead single from *Barrio Fino,* which was the first reggaeton album to reach number one on the Top Latin Album charts. *Barrio Fino,* which remained at number one for an entire year, introduced reggaeton to a legion of followers in the United States, Canada, Europe, and the rest of Latin America beyond the Caribbean.

By the time his follow-up album *El Cartel: The Big Boss* was released in 2007, Daddy Yankee had become a brand name. His image was used to sell soft drinks, footwear, cars, and other products. The singer also starred in the feature film *Talento de Barrio.* Throughout the late 2000s, Daddy Yankee was one of the hottest acts in Latin America, breaking attendance records in Mexico, Ecuador, Bolivia, and elsewhere. In addition to his musical career, Daddy Yankee headed a charity, Corazon Guerrero, which provided food, shelter, and career training to ex-convicts.

In the 1970s, when Jamaican reggae songs were topping the international charts, Panamanians and Puerto Ricans of Jamaican heritage produced their own cross-cultural mix. It was called *reggae en Español,* or Spanish-language reggae. By the early 1990s, Afro-Panamanian artists such as El General and Nando Boom were covering the latest Jamaican dance hall reggae hits, translating the English lyrics into Spanish and singing them over the original rhythms, or "riddims."

One of the most popular riddims was heard on the single "Dem Bow," by Jamaican DJ Shabba Ranks. The simple beat, described by music reviewer Wayne Marshall as "boom-chboom-chick,"[22] was picked up by Puerto Rican hip-hoppers who improvised lyrics over the catchy percussion track. By the mid-1990s, the Puerto Ricans had made what they called *dembow* their own. This became the driving riddim behind reggaeton.

As reggaeton was gaining popularity in Puerto Rico, it was also filtering into cultural melting pots like New York and London. By the early 2000s, the sound was widely dispersed and could be found on popular records by New York-based rapper N.O.R.E. and Puerto Rican reggaeton marvels Daddy Yankee and Tego Calderon. In 2004 Daddy Yankee's pop anthem "Gasolina" became the first international reggaeton hit, appearing on music charts in the United States, Europe, and Canada.

By the time the duo known as Calle 13 appeared on the scene, reggaeton had become one of the most popular styles of Latin music. In 2005 Calle 13 released two singles, "Se Vale Tó-Tó" and "Atrevete-te-te!" which were instant hits on Puerto Rican radio stations. Both songs were included on the group's eponymous debut album *Calle 13*, which won

Calle 13 performs in Argentina in 2009. The Puerto Rican group built a large audience by focusing on humor and social commentary and is among the most popular reggaeton bands in the world.

three Latin Grammys in 2006, including Best New Artist and Best Urban Music Album. The Grammys helped Calle 13 receive significant airplay in the United States, where the group's unique blend of dembow rhythms, hilarious hip-hop lyrics, and fun-filled videos appealed to a wide audience.

Calle 13 differentiated itself from other reggaeton groups through the use of high-tech electronics. The group built its sound with computers, drum machines, electronic vocal effects, and synthesizer keyboards. By the time Calle 13 released its fourth album, *Entren Los Que Quieran*, in 2010, the group was one of the most popular reggaeton bands in the world. It had collected nineteen Grammy awards and sold millions of records focusing on humor and sly social commentary rather than the typical swaggering sex-, drugs-, and violence-based rhymes of other reggaeton artists.

With Calle 13 leading the way, reggaeton continues to evolve. In the 2010s, groups are blending dembow beats and rap lyrics with Caribbean music as various as Jamaican reggae, Dominican merengue, Cuban *son*, and Trinidadian calypso. Meanwhile, new musical ingredients are being added to reggaeton every day, as the style has spread to Venezuela, Colombia, Honduras, and Cuba. Reggaeton has also found receptive audiences in Asia and Africa. Like other Caribbean sounds with roots in past centuries, reggaeton has become an internationally beloved style with a musical reach far beyond its humble roots.

CHAPTER 3

Brazilian Beats

Brazil has the largest black population of any nation outside of Africa, and there are few nations where music is as much a part of the national soul. Brazil's music is heavily influenced by complex African musical traditions that originated with the Yoruba, Fon, Ewe, Bantu, Ashanti, and Hausa peoples. Since the late nineteenth century, these ancient musical roots have merged with indigenous and Portuguese elements to form the modern Brazilian sounds of samba, bossa nova, *tropicália*, and other styles. These genres enjoy international exposure, placing Brazil among the top record-producing nations in the world.

Brazil was settled mainly by the Portuguese rather than the Spanish, which distinguishes it from the rest of Latin America. Consequently, Brazil's nonindigenous people speak Portuguese. The nation is also unique in its celebration of Carnaval, one of the most elaborate and untamed spring festivals in the world. During the six days leading up to Lent, the country shuts down as thousands of costumed celebrants take to the streets to dance, drink, and parade. Samba is the sound track to Carnaval, and this infectious rhythmic sound can be traced back five centuries to a time when Brazil was a nation of black slaves and Portuguese slave masters.

African Roots

The first African slaves were imported to Brazil in 1538. By the time the slave trade ended in 1850, more than 3.5 million Africans had survived the brutal journey across the Atlantic to Brazil—six times more than were taken to the United States. Before slavery was abolished in Brazil in 1888, the country's population included descendants of enslaved peoples from Sudan, Nigeria, Angola, the Congo, and Ghana. These people inherited music, dances, instruments, languages, and traditions from the African continent. This unique Afro-Brazilian culture became intertwined with Amerindian heritage and Portuguese society through intermarriage. By the nineteenth century, most Brazilians were of a multicultural background that blended musical traditions from three continents.

One of those traditions, samba, has its roots in an ancient drumming and circular dance ritual called the *bataque*, originally performed by Brazilian slaves. When a bataque was performed, individuals danced within a circle of vocalists who sang call-and-response lyrics. Spectators and participants kept the rhythm with enthusiastic hand clapping. Although the bataque was originally a religious dance, slaves disguised it as a secular celebration because the Portuguese forbade the Africans to practice their sacred beliefs.

Anti-African prohibitions also forced black Brazilians to disguise their traditional religious practices, merging them with Roman Catholicism. For example, when slaves prayed to a statue of the Virgin Mary, most were actually thinking of the African goddess of the sea, Lemanjá. Prayers to Xangô, the god of fire, thunder, and justice, were represented by the statue of Saint Jerome. This belief system came to be known by the general name of macumba. African drumming and singing were the driving force behind macumba rituals, in which gods were drawn to earth through music in order to answer prayers.

As the population mixed musical and religious practices, both traditions remained alive. World music journalist Chris McGowan and Brazilian sociologist Ricardo Pessanha explain:

Sometimes slaves held drum sessions that on the sur-

Songs of the Wicked *Malandra*

In the 1920s, samba writers often described the antics of lazy street hustlers called *malandros*. The female version of the malandro is the *malandra*. Rejecting the traditional role of a stay-at-home wife and mother, the malandra refuses to cook, clean, or remain true to her mate. Instead, she makes her way in the world by betraying her lovers, flaunting her loose sexual morals, and bragging about a love of black magic and witchcraft. The lyrics of the 1927 "Shantytown Samba" by Sinhô describe a typical malandra:

She fought all the time
But I did nothing to her
And she joined in the orgy
From dusk 'til dawn
And she told everybody

That she was free, that
she was alone
She was the serpent's
daughter
The cobra's granddaughter
I caught her swigging
from a bottle
With the sorcerer
Making witchcraft
With my money
So I packed her bags for her
And sent them to her
To get her own back
She went off to live in the
shantytown.

Quoted in Lisa Shaw. *A Social History of the Brazilian Samba*. Brookfield, VT: Ashgate, 1999, p. 17.

face seemed mere celebrations but in reality were religious rites. And, in turn . . . macumba helped preserve African musical characteristics. African songs, musical scales, musical instruments, and a rich variety of polyrhythms (each deity is called by a particular rhythm and song) have survived in their rituals.[23]

"To Dance with Joy"

Over the course of several centuries, the sacred music of Africa was secularized into several forms. During the eighteenth century, a sensuous Angolan fertility dance called the *lundu* was adopted by members of Portuguese high society. The Portuguese modified the lundu by adding elements of the Spanish fandango. They Europeanized the music by adding refined harmonies along with piano and the Portuguese viola, a fretted guitar-like instrument. In this form, the lundu reigned as the most popular dance in Brazil until the early twentieth century. In 1889 an unnamed author described the lundu:

> The dancers are all seated or standing. A couple gets up and begins the festivity. At the beginning they hardly move; they snap their fingers with a noise like that of castanets, raise or arch their arms, and balance lazily. Little by little, the man becomes more animated: he performs revolutions around his partner, as if he were going to embrace her. She remains cold, disdains his advances; he redoubles his ardor. . . . She moves away, she leaps up; her movements become jerkier, she dances about in a passionate frenzy, while the viola (guitar) sighs and the enthusiastic spectators clap their hands.[24]

As the lundu moved to dance halls patronized by the upper classes, a rowdier music and dance style called the maxixe swept through the slums of Rio de Janeiro. The maxixe merged lundu music with the Brazilian tango, the habanera from Cuba, and the polka, introduced by touring French theater companies. Because it emerged in the steep hillside slums populated by ex-slaves, the maxixe was considered vulgar by Rio's ruling classes. In the early 1900s, parties and dance halls featuring maxixe music were targets for police repression. However, in the slum known as Praça Onze (Plaza Eleven), the maxixe was updated and combined with a style called the *marcha*, which was based on military marching music that featured a fast-tempo one-two, one-two rhythm.

The merging of the maxixe, marcha, and ancient bataque came to be known as samba, and the music followed two distinct paths. In fancy ballrooms, middle-class dancers embraced one another and swirled to the sounds of melodious *samba canção*. This style features sentimental lyrics sung with sophisticated harmonies and backed by stringed instruments, woodwinds, and percussion. In the streets, *samba-enredo* was riotous dance music played primarily on African percussion instruments such as the *agogo*, two metal bells hit with a stick; the single-headed *atabaque* drum; and the *cuica*, a small drum with a stick of bamboo inserted in the head. The cuica is played when the bamboo stick is rubbed with a wet cloth while the drummer manipulates the surrounding drumhead with his fingers. This action produces sounds similar to jungle birds, frogs, and howler monkeys.

Since it was first played in Rio, samba-enredo has emerged as the most popular form of samba. Its intricacies are described by Chris McGowan and Ricardo Pessanha:

> [Samba is] a vibrant musical form distinguished by increased [call-and-response] singing, more emphasis on percussive interplay, and a less formal sound than either maxixe or marcha. Technically, samba has a 2/4 meter with its heaviest accent on the second beat . . . and many interlocking, syncopated lines in the melody and accompaniment. The main rhythm and abundant cross-rhythms can be carried by hand-clapping or in the percussion, which today may be performed by more than a dozen different drums and percussion instruments. Samba is commonly accompanied by the guitar and the four-stringed [ukulele-like] cavaquinho.[25]

In 1917 these elements came together in "On the Phone," the first samba song ever recorded. The lyrics say more about the style, perhaps, than any musical description: "The commandant of fun / Told me on the phone / To dance with joy."[26]

Carnaval *Sambistas*

By the time "On the Phone" was released, samba music and the rowdy spring festival of Carnaval were firmly linked. Although the roots of Carnaval can be traced back to the mid-1500s, the now-famed celebration of Brazil did not emerge until the early 1900s, when the citizens of Rio held two pre-Lent carnivals. One Carnaval appealed to the upper classes, who formed elite groups called *sociedades* to organize dances and costume balls. The sociedades also held annual European-style parades featuring military brass bands,

The Salgueiro samba school takes part in the 2009 Carnaval in Rio de Janeiro, Brazil. Samba schools are found in all the major Brazilian cities and provide year-round employment.

drum bands, and elaborately festooned carriages and floats. Rio's richest men and women attended the parades wearing cat and pig masks.

Poor people, who were mostly black or mulattos of mixed-race heritage, were shut out of these festivities. They initiated their own version of Carnaval, led by aggressive, all-male groups who paraded through the streets of the favelas, or shantytowns, dressed like African warriors. Musicians beat on African drums, and spectators sang the Carnaval anthem "Make Way," with lyrics that state: "Hey, make way / I want to pass / I like parties / I can't deny that."[27]

Individuals called *sambistas* who participated in the favela Carnaval were men who existed on the margins of society, often by illegal means. The samba schools and samba societies they formed to organize and perpetuate their increasingly popular version of Carnaval were often repressed and attacked by authorities.

Sambistas defined their beleaguered lives with samba-enredo lyrics that addressed the discrimination and grinding poverty they faced every day. Songs described or made fun of street violence, prostitutes, and naive peasants from the country who were moving into the city slums. A favorite topic was the *malandro*, a street hustler who abhorred work but loved women, gambling, drinking, and partying. The 1931 song "Cool Mulatto" by Noel Rosa describes a typical malandro:

This strong mulatto
Is from Salgueiro
Hanging around the dry cleaner's
Was his favorite sport
He was born lucky
And since he was a kid
He's lived from a pack of cards
He's never seen a day's work.[28]

Although such lyrics were criticized by Rio's elite, they were extremely popular with average hardworking Brazilians, many of whom envied the lucky gambler in the song. Such songs also helped popularize the raucous version of Carnaval as practiced by the ex-slaves and their descendants.

When a new, more liberal government took over Brazil in 1930, a policy of tolerance was enacted concerning the sambistas. Police no longer harassed samba societies, and the black Carnaval was officially considered *cultura afro-brasileira*, or part of Afro-Brazilian culture. The government was undoubtedly motivated by the fact that Carnaval was attracting an ever-growing number of tourists from around the world, giving the Brazilian economy a much-needed boost. Since that time, Carnaval has grown in scope and importance. Today, the six-day celebration in Rio is ten times bigger than its American counterpart, Mardi Gras in New Orleans. Celebrations in other Brazilian cities such as Salvador, Recife, and São Paulo also attract huge crowds.

Those who participate in Carnaval festivities attend samba schools that are found in every major city. The schools, each with three to five thousand members, are formed by neighborhood groups and include citizens of all ages, from toddlers to senior citizens. Members of samba schools rehearse for Carnaval year-round and hold weekly "samba nights" that are filled with dancing, singing, and band music. These important institutions also provide full-time employment to composers, musicians, and those who construct floats and sew costumes for the annual festival.

The epicenter for Carnaval festivities is the massive 70,000-seat, 766-yard-long (700-meter) stadium called the Sambadrome in Rio, which was built in 1984. During the last two days of Carnaval, attendees pay more than $700 to watch dancers and drummers from dozens of samba schools stage eighty-minute-long parades, each featuring up to five thousand dancers, hundreds of drummers, and dozens of magnificent floats. All are competing to win the title of Carnaval champion. The festivities are televised live and are seen by millions of people worldwide.

Old and New Sounds

Despite the ostentatious glamour of the modern Carnaval, many of Brazil's biggest stars remain true to their more humble roots. The popular singer Paulinho da Viola, for example, forgoes digital keyboards and electric instruments for the traditional samba arrangements featuring guitar, *cavaquinho*, the tambourine-like *pandeiro*, and the *tamborim*, a small, high-pitched Brazilian drum.

Several chart-topping women singers also combine elements of old and new. Clara Nunes was an enormously popular artist who recorded more than sixteen albums of updated samba and pop songs. However, Nunes also sang songs that included religious invocations and lyrics steeped in macumba mythology. Singer Beth Carvalho was known for her repertoire of catchy pop samba songs, but also for her version of samba known as *pagôde*, which features a strong emphasis on African percussion. One of Carvalho's songs, "O Encanto do Gantois," is a tribute to the head priestess of a macumba sect in Salvador.

Alcione, another major female star in Brazil, explores many styles of samba, both old and new, as well as songs with indigenous roots. According to Chris McGowan and Ricardo Pessanha, she "can switch effortlessly between pop romantic ballads perfect for a dark . . . nightclub and folk-

loric excursions that would make an ethnomusicologist leap for his or her tape recorder and notebook."[29] Alcione, along with Carvalho and Nunes, are known as the three Queens of Samba, and their best-selling songs are popular not only in Brazil, but also in Europe, Japan, and the United States.

The New Beat of Bossa Nova

While the wild samba is at the heart of rowdy Carnaval celebrations, it is not the only interpretation of the beat born in Brazil. In the late 1950s, singer-guitarist João Gilberto, a middle-class musician living in the Ipanema beach district of Rio, created a sensation with his version of samba called new beat, or bossa nova.

Gilberto created bossa nova by mellowing the samba rhythm into a laid-back style that could be played by fingerpicking a nylon-string guitar with no other instrumental accompaniment. He sang along to this beat in an exceptionally smooth, quiet vocal style. Gilberto's first recordings of

Beth Carvalho performs at the 2007 Montreux Jazz Festival in Switzerland. She is known for her version of samba called pagôde.

João Gilberto and Stan Getz (left to right) perform in the Rainbow Grill in New York City's Rockefeller Center in 1972. Their successful collaboration inspired dozens of U.S. jazz artists.

the new sound, the songs "Chega de Saudade" and "Bim-Bom," were released in July 1958. Both featured calming, relaxed vocals and unusual harmonies considered off-key by some critics. Despite this view, the songs and a subsequent album by Gilberto kicked off a Brazilian bossa nova craze. Popular artists such as Sergio Mendes, Carlos Lyra, and Nara Leão eagerly capitalized on the fad, releasing albums of both new bossa nova songs and old samba songs played in the new beat style.

In 1964 bossa nova achieved spectacular success on the international scene when Gilberto teamed up with American jazz saxophonist Stan Getz for the Grammy-winning album *Getz/Gilberto*. A single from the album, "The Girl from Ipanema," sung by Gilberto in a bilingual duet with his wife, Astrud, became an international hit, selling more than 2 million copies.

The *Getz/Gilberto* album inspired dozens of American jazz artists to merge the American and Brazilian styles.

Bossa nova was transformed into complex, multilayered music by jazz players such as flutist Herbie Mann, saxophonist Paul Winter, and guitarist Charlie Byrd. Winter comments on this phenomenon: "We were hearing a very gentle voice that had the kind of soul and harmonic beauty that we loved in jazz. . . . [It] was astounding to find a very quiet, gentle music that had an equal amount of magic. It was a whole new possibility for us."[30]

Protest Music in Brazil

In the mid-1960s, the bossa nova style was altered once again when it was combined with rock and roll and protest music into a style called MPB, or *música popular brasileira*. MPB did not have specific musical characteristics, like bossa nova, because it was interpreted differently by each artist. The songs did have common elements, however. MPB combined catchy melodies, vibrant harmonies, Brazilian beats, and rock rhythms with poetic lyrics that called for social justice. The style emerged at a time when a military coup had overthrown the progressive Brazilian government and replaced it with a repressive right-wing regime run by Marshal Humberto de Alencar Castelo Branco and a succession of brutal military dictators.

The MPB singers' style became nationally popular because of televised concerts. These shows featured fierce battles between performers who had to compete with about three thousand entrants before the top twelve were chosen for a televised match. The winners for best compositions, lyrics, musical arrangements, and traditional song interpretations might each receive about $20,000. This was an astronomical sum at a time when the average Brazilian lived on only a few dollars a day. In addition, winners could record albums that might sell more than a hundred thousand copies in a few weeks.

With names such as *Brazil Festival of Popular Music* and the *International Song Festival*, the TV shows became a national craze. On nights when the programs aired, streets, bars, and cafés were empty as millions stayed home to watch the musical battles. There was a political element to

The Jeers of the Audience

When MPB singers competed on popular television shows, they risked alienating their audiences with either mediocre songs or left-wing political views. Performer Sérgio Ricardo did both in 1967, according to Christopher Dunn, the codirector of the Brazilian Studies Council at Tulane University:

> Sérgio Ricardo, a well-known singer-songwriter associated with protest music . . . was initially well received by the audience, but his song "Beto bom de bola" (a song about the travails of a soccer player) failed to satisfy its expectations. On the last evening of the [Brazil Festival of Popular Music], the audience . . . jeered Ricardo when he appeared on stage. Unable to perform his song over the din, he hurled condescending remarks to the audience: "I would ask those who applaud and those who jeer to demonstrate *lucidez* [lucidity] at this moment in order to understand what I'm going to sing." His appeal . . . to legitimize his song and shame critics, further provoked the ire of the audience. After a couple of false starts, he exclaimed: "You won. This is Brazil. This is an underdeveloped country! You're all a bunch of animals!" He proceeded to smash his guitar and hurl it at the audience, precipitating his disqualification from the festival.

Christopher Dunn. *Brutality Garden*. Chapel Hill: University of North Carolina Press, 2001, p. 64.

the competitions as well. When singers injected left-wing political content into their lyrics, those in the audience who supported the government waved flags and loudly booed and jeered them. Meanwhile, supporters tried to drown out the catcalls with loud cheers as singers struggled to sing above the din.

Some of Brazil's most popular MPB singers were those who bravely opposed a government that was notorious for arresting, torturing, and killing dissidents. Singer-songwriter Geraldo Vandré, for example, consistently won competitions with angry lyrics sympathizing with the plight of repressed farmers, workers, and left-wing students. The songs Vandré performed on MPB television shows between 1966 and 1968 also drew the attention of officials, who called his lyrics subversive, offensive to the military, and supportive of illegal student demonstrators. Fearing for his life, the popular singer was forced to leave Brazil in 1969.

Tropicália

Even as some MPB musicians were facing intense pressure from the government, another school of Brazilian music arose that was considered even more radical by authorities. The style, called *tropicália*, was forged among artists, intellectuals, workers, politicians, and activists who opposed the tactics of Castelo Branco and his administration. The tropicália movement coalesced around singers who were saddened by the widespread poverty and repression they

Caetano Veloso and Gilberto Gil perform at the 1994 Vienne Jazz Festival in France. The guitarists introduced the tropicália style, which combines the celebration of Brazilian culture with political and social commentary.

observed in their daily lives. Christopher Dunn, codirector of the Brazilian Studies Council at Tulane University, explains:

> Tropicália was both a mournful critique of [the political] defeats as well as an exuberant, if often ironic, celebration of Brazilian culture and its continuous permutations. As its name suggests, the movement referenced Brazil's tropical climate, which throughout history has been exalted for generating lush abundance or lamented for impeding economic development along the line of societies located in temperate climates. The tropicalists purposefully invoked stereotypical images of Brazil as a tropical paradise only to subvert them with pointed references to political violence and social misery. The juxtaposition of tropical plenitude and state repression is best captured in the phrase . . . "brutality garden" which was taken from a key tropicalist song.[31]

Like MPB, tropicália was first played to a national audience on a televised music competition. In 1967 Caetano Veloso and Gilberto Gil introduced the style, playing songs that combined North American rock, blues, jazz, pop, and psychedelic music with African sounds and Brazilian bossa nova and folk. Many Brazilians disliked this musical amalgamation intensely because rock and roll and electric guitars were disdained by the public in the land of the samba. As cultural revolutionaries, the tropicálists took a measure of glee in offending the public. In 1968, though, Veloso went too far. Appearing at the International Song Festival in plastic clothes with his band the Mutants, Veloso was unable to finish his song "Forbidding is Forbidden" because of the wild booing. Gil went on to face worse problems. In 1969 his songs so irritated Brazil's dictator that he was jailed for a time without ever being charged with a crime. Veloso was also imprisoned for several months in 1969, charged with antigovernment activities. The performer was forced into exile in London upon his release.

The tropicália movement, which encompassed music, film, theater, poetry, and avant-garde art, was brief, lasting only from 1967 to 1969. However, the freedom to experiment exhibited by its musical practitioners opened up doors for other musicians, who began combining rock with traditional Brazilian music. By the mid-1970s, the novel styles that incited violent booing in the 1960s had become part of mainstream Brazilian music. Gil himself continued to experiment, drawing heavily from African music such as juju as well as reggae and funk.

Veloso, too, continued to innovate after he returned to Brazil in 1972. In the 1980s, he began drawing on reggae, samba, and *frevo* from northern Brazil for inspiration. By the 1990s, Veloso and Gil were both major stars in Brazil, along with other former tropicálists such as Gal Costa, Maria Bethânia, João Bosco, and Milton Nascimento.

The music of the tropicálists influenced several generations of musicians in the United States. Rock stars Beck, Nelly Furtado, David Byrne, Kurt Cobain of Nirvana, and Devendra Banhart have all cited tropicália as a major influence. In 1998 Beck released an album titled *Mutations* as a tribute to Veloso's Mutants. One single from the album, "Tropicalia," reached number twenty-one on *Billboard*'s modern rock singles chart. The tropicália movement also inspired countless Brazilian musicians to take an interest in rock-and-roll music.

Rocking in Rio

Tropicália provided a foundation for another style of Brazilian music, tropical rock, which began to emerge in the 1980s. Tropical rock combines American and Brazilian influences with those of British bands like the Beatles and Rolling Stones. The music received a huge boost from the Rock in Rio festival, first held in 1985. The weeklong event, attended by a total of 1.4 million people and broadcast on national TV, featured mega acts such as Queen along with Brazilian performers like Gilberto Gil and rocker Rita Lee. In 2001 Rock in Rio was broadcast in fifty countries. The 2004 version of the festival was even larger, drawing nearly 1.5 million rock fans, who came to hear Britney Spears as well as international rockers like João Pedro Pais and Fattiqueira.

The 2011 Rock in Rio festival was held once again in Rio de Janeiro, Brazil, after traveling to various locations worldwide. It featured Brazilian musicians such as Tony Belloto and Milton Nascimento (left to right).

Between 2004 and 2010, the Rock in Rio festival was held semiannually and locations alternated between Lisbon, Portugal, and Madrid, Spain. In 2011, Rock in Rio 4 was held once again in Brazil. The roster featured some of the best-selling rock and pop acts in the world, including Coldplay, Guns N' Roses, Elton John, Metallica, Red Hot Chili Peppers, Rihanna, Shakira, and Stevie Wonder. Rock in Rio 4 also featured some of Brazil's most famous faces, including Milton Nascimento and a reunion of the Mutants.

Favela Street Beats

Hip-hop music is another American style that has taken hold in Brazil. Like other genres, hip-hop was given its own exceptional imprint by residents of the nation's favelas. In the 1990s, the four-man Racionais MC's was Brazil's best-selling rap act. The group's hard-core rap was inspired by the harsh conditions in the shantytowns of Rio, São Paulo, and Brasília, where the average monthly wage was about $100 and drug lords ruled through violence and murder. Brazilian music journalist Jan Field explains the rise of Racionais MC's: "[They] made their name by performing relentlessly in the favelas and rapping about drug trafficking, racism, and government corruption. Hard-hitting street beats heavy on drums and bass—inspired by

The Sound of Bullets

In 2005 music correspondent Alex Bellos described the danger and excitement he found while attending a funk carioca street party in Rio de Janeiro, Brazil, at 5 A.M.:

In the sultry depths of Rio's Nova Holanda shanty town—or favela—more than 1,000 people are dancing in a narrow street. A wall of speakers stacked 15 feet [4.5m] high and 60 feet [18m] wide sends a dirty, electro beat shuddering through the ground. On a tiny stage, MCs Juca and Paulinho shout out the lyrics of their hit "24 Hours": "Bullets into the Terceiro [a rival street gang]," they chorus. "Shoot the snitch!" Suddenly the crackle of gunfire cuts through the bass: from the middle of the swaying crowd, someone is shooting into the air. . . .

An hour later, as the two MCs leave, the block party is still going strong; Juca and Paulinho pass two teenage boys who are dancing together, waving their automatic pistols in the air. Back in their car, Juca shrugs off the gunfire during the set. Anyone brought up in the favela is used to the sound of bullets, he says. "And anyway, if the guy shoots in the air, it means he likes the song."

Alex Bellos. "Ghetto Fabulous." *The Guardian*, September 17, 2005. www.guardian .co.uk/music/2005/sep/18/brazil.popandrock.

old-school North American rappers like Run-DMC and Public Enemy—back samples and loops of Brazilian popular music."[32]

In 1998 Racionais MC's' album *Sobrevivendo no Inferno* (*Surviving in Hell*) sold more than a million copies, a record number for an independent release in Brazil. Videos for the songs "Diário de um Detento" ("Diary of an Inmate") and "Mágico de Oz" ("Wizard of Oz") received Viewer's Choice Awards from MTV Brazil.

The Anti-Music of Funk Carioca

In the 2000s, the hip-hop beats and raging rap from Rio's favelas evolved into a new style of street music called funk carioca. Although the style was new, it had roots in American recordings from the 1980s and '90s.

The initial inspiration for funk carioca came from a New York group called Afrika Bambaataa and the Soul Sonic Force. The group's 1982 song "Planet Rock" presented a new style of electronic dance music referred to as electro-funk. The sound was achieved by mixing samples from 1970s funk artists like Funkadelic and Sly Stone with beats created on the Roland TR-808 drum machine. The TR-808 was extremely popular in the 1980s and provided the drum sound on numerous hits, including those by Michael Jackson, the Beastie Boys, Dr. Dre, Puff Daddy, and others.

In the early 1990s, electro-funk became the dynamic sound track of Miami's poorest neighborhoods. Inner-city Miami was the home of rappers 2 Live Crew, who took electro-funk and created a new sound called Miami bass. This style included fast dance tempos and explicit lyrics punctuated by electronic stings. The thumping bass drums and hissing cymbals were provided by the TR-808.

The Miami bass sound was a prominent feature of a single called "808 Volt Mix" by American DJ Battery Brain, released in 1993. The song, with rhythms created on the TR-808, was extremely popular among Rio's DJs and was often played at dance parties. Brazilian hip-hoppers soon adapted the singular electro-funk beat from "808 Volt Mix" as a rhythm for obscene Portuguese raps. The 808 rhythms were layered with short samples of Brazilian atabaque hand drums, accordions, and horns. In 2004 the sound was described by Brazilian correspondent Alex Bellos in the British newspaper *The Guardian*:

> The music is called funk, but it's not what a non-Brazilian would understand by that term. There are no over-produced hooks or soulful melodies. Rio funk is a crude collage of Miami bass and rap—a pared-down anti-music made on simple machines, with almost identical rhythms and tunes, no grace of delivery and shouted lyrics, predominantly crude and sexual. . . . The tracks are still made using basic "cut and paste" computer technology in small studios in Rio's suburbs. It uses samples from whatever it likes and piracy is rife.[33]

By the mid-2000s, funk carioca was the sound of choice for gang members and the urban poor in Rio's favelas. DJs like Deize, Serginho, and Marlboro took to writing more socially conscious lyrics, paying homage to those who were jailed or had died in the city's ongoing drug wars.

DJ Gilberto entertains partygoers at a funk dance hall in a Rio de Janeiro favela in 2006. Funk carioca first became popular among the urban poor of Brazil.

Meanwhile, funk carioca concerts were sponsored by drug lords nearly every weekend in the favelas. They featured massive sound systems that attracted thousands of people who danced until dawn.

Like with samba in earlier centuries, the sex and violence associated with funk carioca stirred outrage from Brazilian authorities and media outlets. However, the sound, like samba before it, soon became fashionable among Rio's middle classes after finding a place in the city's upscale nightclubs. Funk carioca was also attracting attention in New York clubs, where the electro-funk sound began. In Europe, the funk carioca song "Follow Me, Follow Me," by Black Alien & Speed became a megahit after it was featured in a Nissan commercial. DJ Marlboro commented on the international popularity of the homegrown Rio sound: "Samba had to go through the same process. Funk [carioca] is finally being perceived as the cultural movement that it is and one of the reasons is that the style is reaching its maturity. We are seeing the boom of a genre now, not just some songs."[34]

From the ancient bataque through samba, MPB, tropical rock, and funk carioca, Brazil's music scene has seen constant change even as the old musical styles have endured. In a nation where music and dance are central to daily life, there is little doubt that the music of Brazil will continue to merge, mutate, and explode onto the airwaves from South America to the United States, Europe, and beyond.

CHAPTER 4

Music of South America

The music of Brazil often overshadows other sounds emanating from South America. Despite the attention paid to Brazilian samba, bossa nova, and other styles, every South American nation has a rich musical history and each country has its own unique styles of music. Like the samba in Brazil, these styles developed with varying degrees of influence from Amerindian, African, and European cultures.

Musicologists divide South America into three zones of cultural influence. The nations of Argentina, Chile, and Uruguay have a dominant Spanish European culture. Bolivia, Paraguay, Ecuador, and parts of Colombia and Venezuela exhibit strong Amerindian influences. The coastal regions tend to have the largest cities and a dominant black influence, sometimes mixed with Spanish elements. Within these zones, smaller subsets have emerged over the centuries, dictated by the multicultural mix of the region.

Cumbia from Colombia

Colombia is a good example of the complex musical geography of South America. The nation is divided into several separate regions, each producing distinct musical styles that evolved from their own unique cultural circumstances. Indigenous music dominates the nation's interior rain forests,

Dancing the *Redondo* in Venezuela

In Venezuela, people of African descent who live in the state of Yaracuy celebrate their patron saint, John the Baptist, with a dance similar to the Colombian cumbia. It is described by ethnomusicologist Max H. Brandt:

> [The] dance requires many people to participate at the same time, usually multiple pairs or three or more people dancing in a line or a circle, each with an arm or a hand on his or her neighbor's shoulder. The *redondos* [round drums] accompany a standard song. . . . [A] man and a woman dance provocatively in circular movements as spectators form a circular arena around them. The dancers' movements and the formation of the onlookers . . . are said to give this drum and its music the name *redondo* ("round").
>
> A rhythm and song known as *malembe* accompanies the street processions with the image of Saint John the Baptist. *Minas* [a type of drum] or *redondos* accompany the *malembes* and processions with a unison rhythm. . . . Though *malembe* means "softly, slowly, take it easy" in various Bantu languages, the people . . . are not aware of its African roots and use it simply as the name of a kind of music.

Quoted in Dale A. Olsen and Daniel E. Sheehy, eds. *The Garland Handbook of Latin American Music.* New York: Garland, 2000, p. 239.

where Amerindians moved to escape Spanish conquest in earlier centuries. Interior valleys contain regions where African influence is strongest because runaway slaves settled there. Along the coasts, the Spanish imprint remains strong.

As in other South American nations, the most popular styles in Colombia are influenced by African rhythms and melodies. Foremost among these genres is the cumbia, a drum-based music and dance style modeled on the *cumbé* from Guinea, where the word means "celebration."

The roots of the cumbia can be traced to the late 1600s, when African and Amerindian slaves gathered to dance and play music on holidays. During those times, the streets filled with people dressed in white. The women wore long, layered skirts, and the men wore red neckerchiefs and carried bundles of flaming white candles.

When a cumbia celebration commenced, revelers formed a large circle. Drummers played complex layered beats featuring three African drums: the *llamador, alegro*, and *bombo* or *tambora*. Women danced flirtatiously in the middle of the circle, enticing the men to draw close, then pushing them away as they advanced. As the volume and intensity of the drumming increased, the men tried to outdo one another, performing increasingly difficult dance moves to win the women's attention. The candles were passed one by one to the females as symbolic floral bouquets.

In later centuries, the cumbia sound changed as it merged with Spanish lyrical song structures and the wistful melodies of Amerindian ballads. The evolution continued as new instruments were added to the traditional African drum and voice arrangements. Those with Amerindian backgrounds brought scrapers, cane flutes, and the *gaita*, a long, sharp-toned flute. Those with Spanish roots played cumbia on guitars and lute-like ouds. European band instruments such as trombones, clarinets, saxophones, trumpets, and accordions were also brought to the mix. Throughout this musical evolution, the cumbia retained the sexual nature of the original dance as macho singers called *parranderos*, or partying men, sang lyrics boasting of their conquests.

As cumbia music grew in popularity, the African rhythms, melodies, and dances associated with the style spread to other nations. In Venezuela, for example, a different style of cumbia is played during feasts celebrating Saint John the Baptist.

A Rolling, Infectious Beat

Although the cumbia's origins are in Guinea, the music has a strong Amerindian influence, unlike other South American styles such as the samba and mambo. Ed Morales describes the 2/4, or one-two, one-two cumbia beat, often likened to riding a horse at a loping trot:

> Its essential elements, the [tambora] drums and enormous gaita flutes, combine to give the music a rolling, infectious . . . beat that seems like a fusion between merengue and reggae, with a similar backbeat that sends it surging forward. . . . The cumbia tempo stresses the upbeat, allowing the cumbia to "float" and giving it a kind of perpetual optimistic lilt.[35]

Although the beat remained the same, the place of the cumbia in Colombian society changed over the years. In the early centuries, the style was considered vulgar and crude, music for slave dances shunned by the descendants of the European ruling class. In 1820, however, as Colombia struggled for independence from Spain, the cumbia came to symbolize liberty, freedom, and the fight against colonialism. By the early years of the twentieth century, cumbia was widely celebrated as the national sound of Colombia.

In the late 1940s, as the Cuban mambo fad was taking New York by storm, Colombian musicians began immigrat-

A folkloric troupe dances the cumbia at a Cartagena, Colombia, park in 2009. The musical style dates to the seventeenth century.

ing to the United States to play cumbia to American audiences. In New York, the sound quickly merged with the Afro-Cuban and Puerto Rican influences that eventually led to salsa in the 1970s.

In Colombia, the 1950s were known as the golden age of cumbia as the sound blended with mambo and big band jazz influences. During this time, a bandleader named Fruko founded a record company, Disco Fuentes, that successfully promoted cumbia artists and records throughout Latin America. One of Fruko's acts, the group La Sonora Dinamita, which featured a strong female lead vocalist, was responsible for popularizing cumbia in Mexico in the 1960s. In the years that followed, cumbia earned the nickname the "mother of Colombian rhythms."[36] The sound attracted millions of fans throughout Latin America, with local styles emerging in Panama, El Salvador, Chile, Bolivia, and Ecuador.

In the 1990s, the group Ivan y Sus Bam Band brought cumbia to the Colombian music television channels MTV Centro and VH1 Latin America. The group's performances featured scantily clad female dancers, a drum machine pounding out a heavy beat, and a large brass section playing cumbia rhythms.

In other incarnations of the traditional sound, musicians fused keyboard synthesizers, sampled sound effects, drum machines, and electric guitars to produce technocumbia. This electonic dance music, which originated in Mexico, became popular in Latin clubs throughout the world.

Colombian Tropipop

By the late 1990s, the evolution of cumbia continued as a new generation created a fresh take on the cumbia sound called tropipop. This radio-friendly sound merged cumbia and a traditional Colombian folk style known as *vallenato*, mixed together with foreign genres such as American pop, salsa, and merengue.

A key element of tropipop, vallenato was born in the nineteenth century in Colombia's Caribbean region. The style originated among farmers who doubled as troubadours.

Carlos Vives, who pioneered the tropipop style, performs at a 2006 benefit concert in Los Angeles, California.

Like American cowboys of the era, the farmers sang the songs to while away the lonely hours, but also to lyrically communicate the latest news and gossip as they traveled from town to town. The vallenato singers accompanied themselves on flutes, guitars, small drums, rhythm scrapers, and accordions.

Vallenato was originally viewed as a crude music played by impoverished farmers, but in the twentieth century, the music became a prominent feature at carnivals, festivals, and parties. As with other forms of music that originated among Latin America's poorest citizens, vallenato was eventually accepted by every layer of Colombian society. In 1968 famed vallenato composer Rafael Escalona created the Vallenato Legend Festival, where folk musicians could compete in musical and lyrical battles. Within a few years, the festival became the largest musical event in Colombia, a status it retains today.

In 1993 Carlos Vives, a singer and well-known Colombian actor, pioneered the tropipop style. Vives had starred in a television series based on the life of Escalona and was so inspired by the role that he formed a band. Vives's second album, *Clásicos de la Provincia*, merged vallenato lyrics with rock and pop music played to Afro-Caribbean rhythms. Although traditionalists criticized the singer's updated sound, the album was a huge hit throughout Latin America and won Best Album at the Billboard Latin Music Awards.

Vives inspired a younger generation of musicians, and by the early 2000s, Colombian acts were drawing international fame playing tropipop music. Mauricio & Palodeagua, which released its first album in 2003, seamlessly blended 1960s rock melodies, bossa nova ballads, cumbia, and other traditional folk styles into a breezy beach sound. In 2006 Fanny Lú, another television star turned tropipop singer, topped Latin music charts in the United States, Colombia, Venezuela, and Mexico. Fanny Lú blends rapid-fire dance beats, slick pop productions, synthesized vocal effects, and lyrics about romance, betrayal, and heartbreak.

The tropipop band Bonka won Colombia's Artist of the Year award in 2003 while its group members were still in high school. Flavored with salsa sounds, brassy horn arrangements, and solid boy band harmonies, Bonka's 2006 debut album *Lo Que Nunca Nos Contamos* made the group one of the top-selling acts in Latin America.

Tango Takes Off

Like Colombia, Argentina has a long musical history built on traditional folk music, African and European influences, and, in recent decades, rock, pop, and electronic music. Argentina's most famous style, tango, emerged in the nineteenth century. Like cumbia in Colombia, tango was a creation of Argentina's poorest citizens.

In the 1880s, the capital city of Buenos Aires was a melting pot of former black slaves, white South Americans, European and Caribbean immigrants, and recently arrived rural Amerindians. The musical influences heard in the city were as diverse as its population. Sounds of flamenco from southern Spain mingled in the streets with Italian accordion melodies, syncopated African and Cuban habanera

Born to Sing Tango

Carlos Gardel is a national hero in Argentina, where he is still revered for his contributions to tango music between 1920 and 1935. His story is told by musician Teddy Peiro and musicologist Jan Fairley:

In Argentina, it was Gardel above all who transformed tango from an essentially low-down dance form to a song style popular among Argentines of widely differing social classes. His career coincided with the first period of tango's Golden Age and the development of *tango-canción* (tango song) in the 1920s and '30s. The advent of radio, recording and film all helped his career, but nothing helped him more than his own voice—a voice that was born to sing tango and which became the model for all future singers of the genre. . . . Everything about Gardel, his voice, his image, his suavity, his posture, his arrogance and his natural machismo spelled tango. . . .

During his career, Gardel recorded some nine hundred songs and starred in numerous films, notably *The Tango on Broadway* in 1934. He was tragically killed in an aircrash in Colombia at the height of his fame, and his legendary status was confirmed. His image is still everywhere in Buenos Aires, on plaques and huge murals, and in record store windows, while admirers pay homage to his life-sized, bronze statue in the Chacarita cemetery, placing a lighted cigarette between his fingers or a red carnation in his buttonhole.

Quoted in Simon Broughton and Mark Ellingham, eds. *World Music: Latin and North America, Caribbean, India, Asia and Pacific.* London: Rough Guides, 2000, p. 307.

rhythms, European polkas, and the lonely country songs of Argentine gauchos, or cowboys.

Buenos Aires was a boomtown, and most of the population was male. This spawned an underworld of cheap bars and seedy brothels. In the early years of the twentieth century, men who lacked female partners practiced dancing with one another. The dances often degenerated into violent competitions with macho, knife-wielding dancers engaging in mock battle. In brothels, the tango took on an air of sexual possession as men danced cheek-to-cheek with prostitutes.

The music of the tango was played on inexpensive instruments, including flutes, guitars, violins, and a concertina-like instrument called a *bandoneón*. In later years, tango bands grew in size to include the upright bass, piano, and several violins and bandoneons.

Considered scandalous and immoral by polite society, the tango remained unknown outside Buenos Aires until an upper-class Argentine writer, Ricardo Güiraldes, described the dance in the 1911 poem "Tango." He wrote that the tango was like the "all-absorbing love of a tyrant, jealously guarding his dominion over women who have surrendered submissively, like obedient beasts."[37] This shocking description helped popularize the tango among the upper classes in Argentine society. In 1912 Güiraldes traveled to Paris, where he thrilled high society with lurid tango demonstrations.

The tango fad soon spread to the United States, where the dance was celebrated in the press, condemned by the clergy, and taught to eager students in hundreds of ballrooms up and down the East Coast. In 1914 New York rabbi Abraham Wise summed up the general attitude of religious authorities toward the tango: "If one were to enter a New York ballroom after a ten years' absence, one would be struck dumb and speechless at the degeneration which has come to pass."[38]

Official scorn did little to quell the fad, and after Hollywood's biggest movie star, Rudolph Valentino, performed the dance in several 1920s films, the tango trend exploded. Between 1920 and 1945, tango was a driving force in the entertainment business. Argentine bandleader Roberto Firpo and singer Carlos Gardel sold hundreds of thousands of tango records and filled ballrooms in Europe, South America, and the United States.

New Tango Styles

Tango rhythms were drowned out by rock and roll in the 1950s. However, the style evolved into the nuevo, or new, tango in the 1960s when bandoneón player Astor Piazzolla added jazz chord structures and rhythms to the traditional tango style. In the 1990s, Argentine musicians melded the traditional tango beat with intricate melodies and digital instruments to produce what is called neo-tango. The Gotan Project, formed in 1999, produced neo-tango layered with samples, bandoneons, violins, cellos, percussion instruments, electronic keyboards, and sound effects like echo and heavy reverb. Their 2008 album, *Gotan Project Live*, features many jam band elements, with songs that are drawn out into extended polyrhythmic grooves filled with musical improvisation.

The eight musicians who make up the group Bajofondo were inspired by the Gotan Project and took the neo-tango sound one step further. Formed in 2002, the originally named Bajofondo Tango Club brought electronic music to the tango jams and created what is called electrotango. The group mixes old and new, blending traditional tango melodies with house music, an electronic genre that often fea-

The Gotan Project (seen performing in 2004) created a neo-tango sound that includes a multitude of instruments and electronic elements.

tures extremely low-pitch, chest-rattling bass lines played on synthesizers. Bajofondo also draws upon mellow, ambient electronica styles called chill out and trip-hop. The group's 2005 album *Remixed* and its follow-up *Mar Dulce* introduced tango to a new generation. Like their great-great-grandparents, tango's latest fans were enamored with the music's rich history and often wicked nature.

The Argentine Beatles

While Argentina is known as the land of the tango, the nation has also produced its share of rock-and-roll bands. The sound dates back to the mid-1950s when the Argentine groups Los Shakers and Los Beatniks first introduced rock music to Buenos Aires audiences. Still, rock music remained overshadowed by the tango until the early 1970s, when pianist and composer Charly García began playing creative and controversial songs.

García was a child prodigy pianist who grew up in a wealthy family in Buenos Aires. Like millions of others who came of age in the 1960s, García was heavily influenced by the Beatles. The Beatles broke up in 1970, but García was inspired to form his own Beatlesque rock band, Sui Generis, in 1972. The group's first album, *Vida*, sold eighty thousand copies, a large number for an unknown band in a nation where most people detested rock and roll.

García called himself the Third World John Lennon, after the outspoken singer-songwriter in the Beatles. Following Lennon's lead, García used his band to push the boundaries of acceptable lyrical content while drawing on his life experiences for inspiration. For example, after he was drafted at the age of twenty, the singer took a large dose of amphetamines and faked a heart attack in order to get expelled from military service. While recovering, he wrote two songs about the experience, "Crazy Boots," about the military, and "Song for My Death," about his drug overdose.

García's next album, *Little Anecdotes About the Institutions*, contained the two controversial songs, along with the antigovernment "John Repression." These songs were censored by Argentina's repressive government, and

Charly García and his band perform in Miami Beach, Florida, in 2012. He is considered one of the most talented and influential artists of Argentine and Latin rock.

the lyrics of another song about censorship itself, "Who Am I Singing For, Then?" also had to be changed.

García quit Sui Generis in 1975, but continued to write controversial lyrics that he put to experimental music. In 1979, he was brought before Albano Eduardo Harguindeguy, the Argentine security minister secretly referred to as the Devil by political resisters. The Devil warned García that if he did not change the political tone of his lyrics, he would be imprisoned. Fearing arrest, García hid his political commentary in abstract lyrics. On his 1980 album *Bicycle*, recorded with his new group Serú Girán, the track "Song of Alice in (Wonder) Land" referenced characters from the Lewis Carroll story to criticize the Argentine military government. Another song, "Meeting with the Devil," slyly referred to the meeting with Harguindeguy. *Bicycle* was a huge success, and the press and public began calling Serú Girán the Argentine Beatles.

Despite the success of Serú Girán's four albums, García left the band and started a solo career in 1982. In the years that followed, García experimented with punk rock, conceptual music, and songs heavily influenced by his experiences with cocaine, whiskey, and other drugs. Although his career had many ups and downs, by 2012 García was considered one of the most talented and influential figures of Argentine and Latin rock.

Los Fabulosos Cadillacs

Charly García's impact was felt across the entire rock spectrum in Argentina and he was a major influence on rock acts that emerged in the 1980s and '90s, including Los Pericos, Soda Stereo, and Sumo. These groups drew upon political events and personal misfortunes for lyrical inspiration. Like García, they were unafraid to mix musical styles.

The nine-piece Los Fabulosos Cadillacs from Buenos Aires was one of the most renowned and influential rock bands in Latin America. The group formed in 1985 and quickly expanded its fan base with a blend of rock, rap, ska, reggae, and traditional South American sounds. In 1995 the group solidified its reputation as South America's premier rockers when it recorded *Rey Azucar* with a host of international stars, including Rubén Blades, Celia Cruz, Mick Jones of the Clash, and Debbie Harry, formerly of Blondie. Los Fabulosos Cadillacs released more than a dozen well-received albums before officially calling it quits in 2002. The group reunited in 2008 after the death of longtime percussionist Gerardo "Toto" Rotblat, releasing two new albums in two years, *La Luz del Ritmo* and *El Arte de la Elegancia de LFC*.

Los Fabulosos Cadillacs was among dozens of Argentine rock bands reinventing the sound of rock for Latin American audiences during the late 1990s and early 2000s. Meanwhile, in the suburbs of Buenos Aires, a new style, appropriately called suburban rock, emerged. This stripped-down, unpretentious sound was similar to American alternative rock played by popular 1990s groups like Nirvana and R.E.M. The blues-based sound of the British rock group the Rolling Stones was also a major inspiration for many suburban rockers. One of the most popular groups, the Ratones Paranoicos, delivered an uncanny imitation of

The Argentinian band Los Fabulosos Cadillacs attends a promotional event for their 2008 concert series in Mexico City.

the Stones's sound but played original music with Spanish lyrics.

By the late 2000s, Argentina had produced rockers who specialized in punk, heavy metal, and techno-pop, while others mixed a variety of genres. The group Karamelo Santo, for instance, brought together Jamaican ska, rock, cumbia, and what the band calls Afro-Uruguayan rhythms. Another one of Argentina's most popular rock bands of the 2000s and early 2010s, Babasónicos, were known to play funk, psychedelic rock, pop, and alternative.

Songs of Resistance

Twenty-first-century Argentine rock groups are free to play and sing whatever inspires them, but this was not always the case. Until the 1990s, a series of brutal dictators silenced musicians with censorship and threats of arrest. The leaders understood well the power of music to rally the public against cruel government policies. The situation was worst in countries like Chile, where those who committed the crime of criticizing dictators in song were imprisoned, tortured, and killed.

Despite such repressive measures, musicians who put their grievances into verse and melody were following an old Latin American tradition. For centuries, folk songs guardedly poked fun at those in power or criticized the status quo. In the 1960s, however, a type of music, *nueva canción*, or "new song," dispensed with subtlety and openly questioned the legitimacy of the government.

Nueva canción, most often associated with Chile, actually began in Argentina as a reaction to the dominance of tango in the national culture. The first nueva canción singers were simply interested in reviving the songs played by downtrodden farmers and workers who were said to preserve admirable traditions of music and culture. Nueva canción songs, therefore, focused on the thoughts and emotions of average citizens while criticizing materialism and progress.

When the new song movement was adopted in Chile, singers felt that it was their obligation to influence the politics of the country to improve the lives of working people. This meant writing songs critical of the small group of corrupt Chilean military authorities who controlled nearly all of the nation's wealth. In this unequal society, the populace was purposefully denied educational opportunities and economic advancement. Jan Fairley, a journalist who specializes in Latin American music, describes how the nueva canción artists responded to Chile's politics:

> With voice and guitar, they composed songs for their own hopes and experiences in places where many of those involved in the struggles for change regularly met and socialized. It is a music that . . . [used the] guitar as gun and song as bullet. Yet the songs—poems written to be performed—are classic expressions of the years of hope and the struggle for change, and their beauty and truth nurtured those suffering under dictatorship or forced into exile. They are still known by heart by audiences throughout the continent and its exile communities.[39]

The first well-known nueva canción artist in Chile was Violeta Parra, born in 1917. Her early musical career was based on playing traditional Chilean songs. In the 1950s, she traveled through the countryside seeking out unrecorded folk songs composed by *payadores*, rural Amerindian poets who followed ancient musical traditions. Parra played the collected songs on radio shows and began to write lyrics

Mercedes Sosa and Argentinian Nueva Canción

The nueva canción style popular in Chile has roots in Argentina, where singer Mercedes Sosa is considered the godmother of the "new song" style. Sosa was born in 1935 and began her singing career at age fifteen. Known for her rich, expressive voice, Sosa followed the nueva canción tradition of speaking truth to power. In the late 1970s, Sosa was the leading public voice criticizing Argentina's ruthless military dictator Jorge Rafael Videla. In 1979 she was arrested during a concert and briefly jailed along with two hundred audience members. After receiving numerous death threats, Sosa moved to Paris, then Madrid. After Videla's regime collapsed in 1982, Sosa returned to Argentina in triumph, recording numerous albums in the years that followed. In the 2000s, Sosa recorded three Grammy-winning albums: *Misa Criolla, Acústico*, and *Corazón Libre*.

In 2009 Sosa received multiple Grammy nominations for her final album *Cantora*. She died soon after at the age of seventy-four. At the time of Sosa's death, Argentina was ruled by the democratically elected Néstor Kirchner, who ordered three days of national mourning. Long after Argentina's brutal military dictator had been consigned to history, tens of thousands of grieving fans viewed Sosa's body as it lay in state at the National Congress building in Buenos Aires.

similar to those she heard from the payadores. These songs served as the foundation of the nueva canción movement. Parra not only appreciated the poetry of Amerindians, but she was also the first to popularize their instruments on the radio. Her backup band used a bamboo flute, or quena, and a small ten-string lute with a body made from an armadillo shell.

Despite her musical success, Parra suffered from depression, and the last song she wrote before committing suicide in 1967 was the whimsical "Thanks to Life" ("Gracias a la Vida"). This song and others composed by Parra have lived on, and her music has been covered by many popular artists, including American folk singer Joan Baez.

"No Revolution Without Song"

The nueva canción style performed by Violeta Parra was popular during an era when millions of Chileans were striving to replace their repressive government with democratically elected officials. In 1965 the center for this movement in the capital city of Santiago was the folk club Peña de los Parra, opened by Parra's children, Angel and Isabel. The club served as a meeting place where activists could hear the music of the popular nueva canción musician Victor Jara.

Jara had sterling credentials to lead Chile's nueva canción movement. He grew up in a squalid shantytown outside of Santiago and survived by helping his mother sell food from a tiny stall downtown. Jara created controversy beginning with his first public performances. One song charged the minister of the interior with ordering the slaughter of impoverished farmers in southern Chile. Other Jara songs were drawn from the singer's own experiences and focused on the harsh realities of life, death, and lost love in Santiago's shantytowns.

Jara was extremely popular, and his music was at the forefront of democratic change in Chile. In the late 1960s, the singer was a driving force behind the Popular Unity Party, whose candidate, Salvador Allende, was elected president in 1970. At a celebratory concert in Santiago, Jara appeared onstage with Allende and other nueva canción musicians under a banner that read: "There Can Be No Revolution Without Song."[40]

Allende's democratic revolution did not last long. On September 11, 1973, the president was murdered during a coup d'état led by army general Augusto Pinochet, who installed a military dictatorship. Five thousand people formerly associated with Allende, including Jara, were arrested and taken to a downtown soccer stadium. Jara was then sent to jail, where he wrote the words to the haunting poem "Chile Stadium."

The next day Jara was taken back to the stadium, where soldiers used rifle butts to break his wrists and hands. Finally, he was shot with a machine gun. His bullet-riddled body was dumped with dozens of others near a local cemetery, and a mortuary worker who recognized him reported his death.

After Jara's demise, the Pinochet government worked to repress the new song movement. Jara's records and those of others were confiscated, and the music was banned from the radio. Anyone caught playing or listening to nueva canción could be arrested, tortured, or killed. Despite these measures, nueva canción survived.

Pinochet was removed from office in 1990, making the political style of nueva canción no longer necessary. Yet the use of traditional instruments and socially relevant lyrics remains popular in Chile and elsewhere. Jara became a musical martyr, and the stadium where he was viciously murdered was renamed Estadio Víctor Jara in 2003.

In the years since Jara's death, his songs have been recorded by folk singer Pete Seeger, as well as rock musicians Jackson Browne, Bob Dylan, Bruce Springsteen, and Sting. In Chile, the old nueva canción from the 1960s and '70s is considered by some to be nearly as important as Chile's national anthem.

In Chile, Argentina, Colombia, and elsewhere throughout South America, homegrown music has long acted as

Victor Jara, the leader of the Chilean nueva canción movement, drew from his own personal experiences to write songs aimed at social and political change.

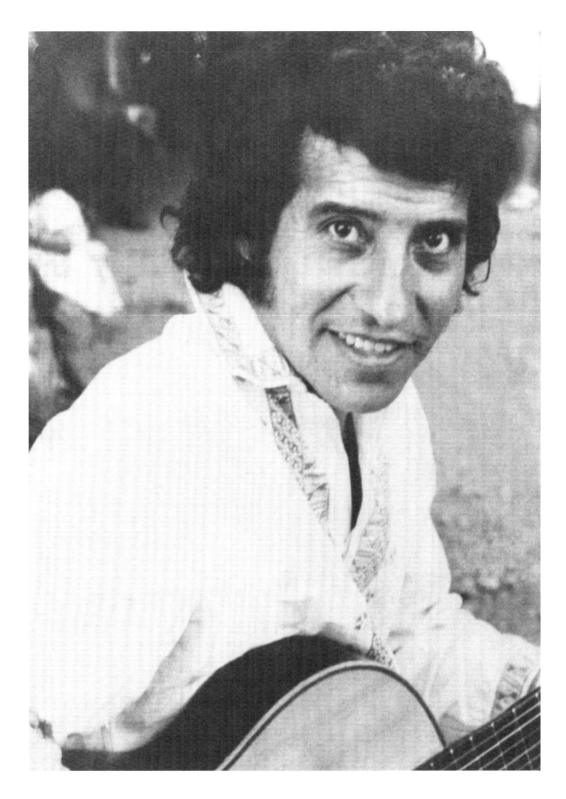

a wellspring of hope, culture, patriotism, and romance. Whether it was played in dance halls or sung to challenge a deadly dictator, South American music, with its roots in African, European, and Amerindian song, helped write the history of a large and diverse continent.

CHAPTER 5

Mexican Music in Two Nations

Until the sixteenth century, the music of Mexico was played by Aztec and Maya musicians. When their society was colonized by the Spanish, elements of their musically advanced sounds remained alive among their descendants. Today about three-quarters of Mexicans are mestizos—people of mixed European and Native American ancestry—and the musical roots of the indigenous Mesoamericans can be heard in Mexican styles ranging from traditional folk songs to *techno-banda*, *corrido*, and *nortec*.

Each region of Mexico has its own unique blend of cultural influences. In southern states, traditional music has a strong Amerindian flavor, while in the central regions, European harps are played with African rhythms. Musicians in northern Mexico and the U.S. border areas play a cornucopia of styles, with Spanish martial horns influencing mariachi and *banda* music, European polkas driving *norteño*, and American pop and rock and roll spicing Tejano and other forms. As Dale A. Olsen and mariachi musician Daniel E. Sheehy write: "[Modern] descendants of ancient Amerindian cultures, rural-rooted mestizo traditions, African-derived traits, and international urban popular music exist side-by-side, giving rise to new musical hybrids."[41]

This musical fusion thrives in Mexico thanks to a large, influential community of young people who dictate musical tastes not only for the entire nation, but all of Central America. Mexican listeners also support a burgeoning entertainment industry that promotes the products of the music business on television and radio. In addition, the border that Mexico shares with the United States has long allowed people and musical ideas to flow between Mexico, California, Texas, and other American states. In 2012 regional music from Mexico comprised more than 60 percent of total Latin record sales in the United States.

Son Songs in Mexico

While modern Mexican music has a variety of influences, its roots are in the *son* style derived from a blend of Spanish, African, and Amerindian elements. This form of Mexican music evolved independently from Cuban *son*.

There are eight different styles of Mexican *son*, some more popular than others. Although the musical forms are different, they all developed in rural areas where audiences participate in foot-stamp dancing, or zapateado. When performing the zapateado, participants drive the heels of their shoes and boots into the dance floor, pounding out a fast counter-rhythm to the musical beat in a way that adds tension and excitement to the music. One of the most famous zapateados is the *jarabe tapatío*, or Mexican hat dance, from Guadalajara, Jalisco. This dance, in which men wear the costumes of the Jalisco cowboy, or *charro*, and the women wear handwoven shawls and colorful sequined skirts, is the national dance of Mexico.

Son audiences help shape the lyrical makeup of songs. As vocalists sing, audience members shout out comments from the dance floor. Singers are expected to respond immediately with clever and amusing lyrics, and those who fail are jeered. Musicians depend on this interaction, adding fanciful flourishes on the violin or guitar to accompany the improvised lyrics.

Individual *son* styles are defined by their instrumentation and musical traditions. For example, *son jarocho* from Veracruz features a thirty-two-string harp that plays a melody. The harp is accompanied by a shallow-bodied guitar

Beating Harps and Dancing Horses

There are many unique, localized versions of Mexican son music, but one of the most unusual comes from the Michoacán region. In this area, which is called "Hell's Waiting Room" because of its hot climate, local people enjoy son de arpa grande, *or* son *of the big harp. Bands that play this style feature two guitars, two violins, and one big harp. The performance style is described by Latin American music scholar Mary Farquharson:*

> The style involves the sound boxes of the big harps being beaten in counter-rhythm by one of the musicians of the band, or by a local fan who pays for the privilege. The harpist, meanwhile, must hold on to the melody—and his harp—delivering a vocal line that can sound something like a shout from the soul.
>
> This style of son used to thrive at country fairs, and urban brothels, but today, the audience are the locals who organise parties on the small farms far from the city, or wealthy stable-owners who pride themselves on their dancing horses. The horses will apparently only dance to the big harp music and they do so on wooden platforms, beating out rhythm and counter-rhythm with their hooves.

Quoted in Simon Broughton and Mark Ellingham, eds. *World Music: Latin and North America, Caribbean, India, Asia and Pacific*. London: Rough Guides, 2000, p. 468.

called a *jarana*, used to strum rhythmic chords, and a small, four-stringed guitar called a *requinto*, on which fast-paced improvised riffs are played. In southern Veracruz, where harps are not common, a different style of son jarocho features guitars of various sizes along with the *pandeiro*, an eight-sided drum with small metal jingles like a tambourine.

Another form of *son* originated among the Zapotec Indians in Oaxaca. Called *son istmeño*, the style features romantic lyrics and is played in a slow, melancholy 3/4 waltz time. The haunting istmeño songs of love and loss have been adapted by non-Indian singers who have learned the Zapotec language to add authenticity to their renditions. One of the most popular urban vocalists in this style is Lila Downs, who is half Amerindian and half American.

Son arribeño is a form especially beloved by country people in the rural regions of central Mexico. The music is played by two *trovadores*, or troubadours, backed by a band featuring two violins, a large eight-string guitar called a *huapanguera*, and a small five-string guitar called a *vihuela*. The singers improvise lyrics about poverty, politics, and the difficulties of making a living from the land. When performing, the musicians compete with one another, as Latin American music scholar Mary Farquharson explains: "Two trovadores . . . confront each other on tall bamboo platforms erected on the sides of a village square. According to an established structure, they enter into musical combat, improvising verses which are interspersed with zapateado dancing."[42]

Mariachi from Jalisco

The most popular form of *son* is mariachi music. It is also called *sones jaliscienses*, or *sons* from Jalisco, the state where the music originated in the mid-nineteenth century. Mariachi bands can have up to twenty players, but all feature at least two violins, two trumpets, one Spanish guitar, one vihuela, and a *guitarrón* (a jumbo acoustic bass guitar).

Mariachi music was originally played at weddings, and some say the name is a corruption of the French word for marriage. The music moved beyond wedding celebrations in the early twentieth century, when unemployed musicians tried to earn a living traveling from village to village to sing songs about love affairs, revolutionary heroes, and current events.

In the 1930s, mariachi became the national sound of Mexico, when it was popularized by radio stations and re-

cord companies. Movies were responsible for making mariachi popular throughout the world. In the 1940s and '50s, the golden age of mariachi, the band Mariachi Vargas de Tecalitlán appeared in more than two hundred Mexican films shown throughout Latin America. North of the border in Hollywood, California, the band was featured in dozens of movies. This group, said to be among the best of the mariachi bands, is still playing today. Although the original players have all died, the personnel of the band is constantly updated with Mexico's most talented musicians.

Mariachi Vargas performs at the 2008 Latin Grammys. The band has been performing for six decades, and its lineup has been continually updated with Mexico's most talented musicians.

Ranchera Country

Mariachi singers often sing popular songs in the *ranchera* style. Ranchera first emerged in the 1930s, when millions of Mexican peasants moved from rural areas to large cities. These people were forced off the land by economic hardship, and they often grew nostalgic for country life as they struggled to survive in Mexico City, Tijuana, and elsewhere. Ranchera singers responded by writing country songs about the natural world, lost love, and the simple life on rancheros, or ranches.

Ranchera songs are played in several tempi, including slow waltzes in 3/4 time, fast polkas in 2/4 time, and boleros in 4/4 time. Musicians play ranchera on guitars, horns, guitarróns, and accordions. In the 1940s, this style was popularized by José Alfredo Jiménez, who wrote and recorded more than four hundred ranchera songs. One of Mexico's most famous ranchera stars, Juan Gabriel, was born in Michoacán in 1950. He began singing and writing original ranchera songs at the age of thirteen, and by the 2010s, he had sold more than 30 million records throughout Latin America.

In the 2010s, Pepe Aguilar has been one of the most popular singers of ranchera and mariachi. Aguilar, born in San Antonio, Texas, in 1968, is the son of Mexican music and film icon Antonio Aguilar. Although he began his musical career as a teenager in a rap band, the younger Aguilar did

Pepe Aguilar, one of the most popular ranchera and mariachi singers, performs at the 2011 Latin Grammys.

not gain widespread notice until he released his 1998 album *Por Mujeres Como Tú*, which spent more than a year on the *Billboard* charts and went multiplatinum, selling 2 million copies worldwide. The following year, Aguilar's *Por Una Mujer Bonita* won a Latin Grammy for Best Album.

Aguilar went on to win nine more Grammys and achieve fame on both sides of the border. In 2002 he was the first singer of Mexican descent to perform at the Hollywood Bowl in Los Angeles. The following year, more than twenty thousand people attended a Los Angeles ceremony where Aguilar was presented with a key to the city. By 2012, Aguilar had released sixteen studio albums. That year, he was awarded a star on the Hollywood Walk of Fame next to the star honoring his father.

Ranchera Women

Unlike mariachi music, which is largely played by men, ranchera has long been popular with Mexico's most famous female singers, called divas. In the 1920s, Lucha Reyes was the first ranchera singer to achieve international fame, performing in several movies and playing in Mexico, Los Angeles, and Europe. In recent years, diva Astrid Hadad has stimulated renewed interest in Reyes's music by recording some of her classic songs.

In 2012 the Latin Grammy nominations for Best Regional Mexican Album were dominated by female ranchera singers. Four-time Grammy winner Paquita la del Barrio (Franny from the Neighborhood) was nominated for her hit single "Eres Un Farsante" ("You Are a Fraud"). Like many other Paquita songs, this one chastises a deceitful man and expresses strong criticism of Mexico's sexist male culture. This topic is also addressed in Paquita songs like "Human Scum," "Like a Dog," and "Two-Footed Rat." To make sure the men in her concert audiences get the message, Paquita often shouts out, "Are you listening, good-for-nothing?"[43]

Another Grammy winner, the all-female ensemble Mariachi Divas de Cindy Shea, covers a wide spectrum of styles. Founded in 1999 by trumpeter Shea, the ensemble plays ranchera, mariachi, and even multiplatinum pop

Paquita la del Barrio, seen here in 2010, criticizes sexist culture with her songs and performances.

covers such as Whitney Houston's "I Will Always Love You." The group picked up a Best Regional Mexican Album Grammy in 2008 for *Canciones de Amor* and won again in 2012 for *Orale*.

Musical Newspapers

Ranchera is among several styles that arose in the rural countryside and continues to enjoy significant popularity. Music known as corrido also originated among impoverished peasants, but the lyrics do not focus on ranchera-style sentimentality and nostalgia. Corrido is a type of protest music meant to agitate and annoy government officials.

The widespread appreciation of corrido first came about between 1910 and 1920, when Mexico was undergoing a bloody political revolution against authoritarian government leaders. In this era, newspaper and radio content was strictly controlled by government and business. The only way for average people to voice their opinions about war, unemployment, and their struggles against powerful land-owners was through corrido lyrics. Because of their content, corridos were originally known as musical newspapers, but rather than relate straight news, the songs used commentary to interpret, celebrate, and honor the subjects of the song.

In its standard form, corrido contains long strings of quatrains, or four-line verses. At the beginning of the song, the singer gives a salutation and provides a prologue, or introduction, to the rest of the verses. The second part of the corrido tells a story of current events. The song often ends with a moral lesson and a farewell from the singer. Unlike the emotional singing style used in ranchera, corrido singers, or *corridistas*, use straightforward delivery so that the verses may be clearly understood by the listener. Corrido is mainly played in 3/4 time and is an accordion-based style most often accompanied by guitars and light percussion.

Glorifying Banditos

In the early days of corrido, Mexican revolutionaries like Francisco "Pancho" Villa were revered as heroes by corridistas even as they were condemned as outlaws by authorities. This tradition of glorifying banditos remains alive in modern times. Today, corrido singers from northern Mexico, called norteño musicians, compose songs to celebrate the deeds of drug lords and narcotics traffickers. These songs, called *narcocorridos*, are heavily criticized in the press and banned from the airwaves in Mexico, but they are extremely popular with young Spanish-speaking audiences on both sides of the Mexico-United States border.

Los Tigres del Norte was one of the first bands to record best-selling narcocorrido songs. The group was formed in 1970 in Sinaloa, a state in northern Mexico, by accordionist Jorge Hernández, his two brothers Raúl and Hernan, and their cousin Oscar Lara. When the band moved to San Jose, California, in the early 1970s, the police called them the Little Tigers, providing a basis for their name.

The first hit for Los Tigres del Norte, "Contrabando y Traicion" ("Contraband and Betrayal"), was recorded in

1972. During this era, before the advent of gangsta rap and hip-hop, this song about marijuana smugglers was extremely controversial. The controversy drew attention to "Contrabando y Traicion," and it quickly became a major Latin hit. Los Tigres del Norte went on to achieve phenomenal success with other modern corrido songs about drug runners and the travails of illegal immigrants. The band also inspired countless other narcocorridos romanticizing the violent and financially rewarding *narco* lifestyle.

Los Tigres del Norte sold records on both sides of the border for decades. The group's hit 1989 album *Corridos Prohibidos* is filled with gloomy Spanish lyrics that betray the bubbly accordion-based sound of the music. Songs on *Corridos Prohibidos* describe a violent world dominated by dangerous men. The song "La Camioneta Gris" describes how a drug-running couple die under the wheels of a train while running from soldiers. "El Zorro de Ojinaga" is about Pablo Acosta, who supplied one-third of the cocaine in the United States during the 1980s before dying during a raid by the FBI.

Los Tigres del Norte remained popular well into the new millennium, and in 2011, their hit "Somos Mas Americanos" ("We Are More American") proved the group was as relevant as ever. The lyrics are delivered from the point of view of an undocumented immigrant in the United States. He reminds listeners that California, Texas, Arizona, and New Mexico were once part of Mexico. The singer states that he is a hardworking man who is considered an invader in a land that once belonged to his native country.

"Somos Mas Americanos" and eleven other best-selling hits were played by Los Tigres del Norte on the TV show *MTV Unplugged* in 2011. The band was joined by musical guests including reggaeton stars Calle 13, Argentinean pop rocker Andrés Calamaro, and Zack de la Rocha, formerly of the rap-metal band Rage Against the Machine. The album, *MTV Unplugged: Los Tigres del Norte and Friends*, was later released.

In 2012 Los Tigres del Norte celebrated their fortieth anniversary, having recorded more than 500 songs on some 50 albums, and selling more than 32 million records

Corrido of the Mexican Revolutionary

The Mexican revolutionary hero Francisco "Pancho" Villa was assassinated by unknown assailants in 1923. The song "Corrido Historia y Muerte del Gral Francisco Villa" ("Corrido History and Murder of General Francisco Villa"), excerpted below, was composed only sixty days after the event. The corrido was used to take the news of Villa's death to villagers throughout the Mexican countryside.

> In a hacienda in my country,
> marvelous México,
> from a worker of the land
> the great General Villa was born....
> He joined Madero's forces
> with a strong hand,
> and the once lowly farmworker
> became an undefeated rebel.
> Due to his extraordinary bravery
> and unsurpassed fierceness,
> at Rellano Don Pancho (Madero)
> promoted him to the rank of
> general. . . .
> But envy and treachery
> lurked nearby
> waiting for the opportunity
> to take his life.
> Near Parral,
> the motive has yet to be discovered,
> they killed the General
> as he was driving his automobile....
> His soldiers grieved for him
> because he was their hope,
> and the brave Dorados
> swore to avenge his death. . . .
> May you rest in peace, because
> your name
> shines like a star in history:
> immortal will be the fame
> of General Pancho Villa.

Vivo. "Corrido Historia y Muerte del General Francisco Villa." *The Mexican Revolution: Corridos About the Heroes and Events 1910–1920 and Beyond!* (CD7041-7044). Arhoolie Records, 1996. http://artsedge.kennedy-center.org/interactives/lessons/corridos/corridos.swf.

---

worldwide. The band, which has been credited with turning norteño music into an international genre, continues to expand its musical repertoire, updating its sound with elements of rock, cumbia, and attention-grabbing effects such as machine guns and sirens.

The Banda Boom

Norteño is among the many styles played by bandas, groups that feature trumpets, trombones, saxophones, tubas, clarinets, and percussion instruments such as the tambora

In recent years, banda music has increased greatly in popularity. Groups such as Banda El Recodo, which was founded in 1938, regularly fill stadiums.

drum. Banda music, heavily influenced by polka, has roots in nineteenth-century Sinaloa. Today, banda is played by groups of six to twenty musicians, who perform rancheras, corridos, narcocorridos, cumbias, and boleros.

Banda music has exploded in popularity throughout Mexico, where it is a staple on radio and television. Concerts by groups such as Banda el Recodo fill stadiums, while nearly every small village hosts a banda concert each weekend. The banda craze has also created new dance fads such as the quebradita, described as an acrobatic combination of the polka, lambada, cumbia, and jitterbug.

While banda has traditionally been the premier music style of Mexico, its status was challenged in the 1980s and '90s by a new brand of banda called *techno-banda*. This modernized version of the sound replaced horns with digital synthesizers and the electric bass with a tuba. At clubs, the sound was typically blasted through tooth-rattling

Battle of the Bandas

As the digitized sound of techno-banda grew in popularity in the 1990s, it displaced established banda groups that played the traditional style. The battle between banda and techno-banda is described by Latin music professor Helena Simonette:

> When technobanda hit Southern California in the early 1990s, there was no question among banderos [banda musicians] working in the Los Angeles area that this new musical trend would have a lasting impact on their own music, their repertory, as well as their economic situation. . . . The clarinetist and bandleader Felipe Hernández, who settled down in Los Angeles in the 1980s, summarized technobanda's influence on the local Sinaloan banda: "The techno-banda movement did not help *banda sinaloense* at all. . . . [The] only thing they accomplished was to ruin what we used to earn. They are six or seven musicians, we are a banda of fifteen. When I formed my banda, I charged $1,500–1,600 for two sets. Nowadays they pay me $800. Why? Because when [the technobandas] came out, it was what people liked. If they get $100 for each [musician], that's a good salary." . . . Relying on synthesizer and electric instruments, technobanda was able to downsize its ensemble to half or a third of the personnel of an acoustic banda.

Helena Simonette. *Banda: Mexican Musical Life Across Borders.* Middletown, CT: Wesleyan University Press, 2001, pp. 263–264.

sound systems. Groups that played techno-banda were limited to seven or eight members, but also featured vocalists, who played only minor roles in traditional banda. The smaller bands were cheaper for promoters to hire and, for a time, the popularity of techno-banda surpassed traditional banda.

Despite its temporary success, the status of techno-banda faded in the 2000s. In Southern California, traditional banda became fashionable again, but this time with a new twist—a growing appreciation for the lead tuba. Although the honking bass tuba was previously shunned by young immigrants, banda groups with tuba players were suddenly in demand at nightclubs and house parties across the Los Angeles basin. As *Los Angeles Times* reporter Sam Quinones wrote in 2011:

> No longer forced to the back of the *banda*, tuba players are out front, standing next to singers, leading lines through parties. They are showing their chops with wild improvisation while keeping time and bass to traditional three-chord Mexican songs. . . . Today, the thunder of *banda* tuba experimentation peals across Southern California, with players using hip-hop, country, scratching, jazz and electric bass lines as they reinvent a Mexican folk music far from home.[44]

Mexican American Rock and Roll

The banda boom is only one example of musicians in the United States drawing from the musical styles of Mexico. Hispanic musicians have also played an important role in shaping American pop and rock and roll. In the seminal days of rock in the late 1950s, one of the style's biggest stars was Mexican American Richard Valenzuela, known as Ritchie Valens. Although he was born in Los Angeles, Valens often traveled to Mexico, where he first heard the three-hundred-year-old folk song "La Bamba." Valens recorded the song with a rock tempo and an Afro-Cuban drum. Valens did not speak Spanish and sang the lyrics phonetically.

In 1958 "La Bamba" became the first Spanish-language record to reach number one on the *Billboard* charts in the

Ritchie Valens had the first Spanish-language record to reach number one on the Billboard *charts.*

United States. After "La Bamba," Valens was set to become the biggest Mexican American rock star in history, but his career was cut short after he had been on the national scene for only eight months. A small airplane that was transporting him from a concert in Iowa crashed on February 3, 1959, killing Valens along with rock sensation Buddy Holly.

Valens was among several Mexican American acts that produced classic songs that are still heard on oldies radio stations today. A band called the Champs had a huge hit with the song "Tequila," which was on the charts for nineteen weeks in 1958. The saxophonist for the Champs, Chuck Rio, was a Latino musician from Texas whose Afro-Cuban lead melody helped the song win a Grammy in 1958. "Tequila" was popularized again in the 1980s by Paul Reubens's comedic character Pee-wee Herman and is still played by countless bands today.

The Latin influence on rock and roll continued into the 1960s when Mexican American rock bands began using the electronic Farfisa organ instead of the accordion. The sound of the Farfisa is often described as "cheesy" by music critics, but the organ has a distinctive sound that propelled rock-and-roll songs such as "96 Tears" by Mexican American rockers Question Mark and the Mysterians. As Ed Morales writes, the organ was more than a melody instrument in the hands of Mysterian keyboardist Bobby Balderrama:

> 96 Tears uses the organ as a percussive instrument, the way Afro-Cuban music does, building to an other-worldly, moody apotheosis [peak], especially when combined with [drummer Robert Martinez's] eerie vocals. The Mysterians' music seemed to announce that as Mexican-Americans, they felt like aliens.[45]

"96 Tears" was among several mid-sixties hits by Hispanic artists. Songwriters Chan Romero and Chris Montez wrote several songs that were huge in the 1960s, including "Hippy Hippy Shake," which was recorded by the Beatles and other acts. In 1965, Cannibal & the Headhunters, from East Los Angeles, had a Top 40 hit with their now-classic "Land of 1,000 Dances." Writing about the Mexican American influence on classic rock, Morales states:

> The legacy laid down by Ritchie Valens and the Chicano rockers of the early 1960s was at the root of an entire branch of American rock history, one that many consider to be the most authentic "American" do-it-yourself style. . . . [Genres] popularized in the early to mid '60s, such as frat rock, party rock, and garage rock, and possibly surf music, all sounds that immediately preceded or developed in tandem with the Beatles . . . were at least partly grounded in the hybrid Mexican-American cultures that had already absorbed Afro-Cuban music through Mexico's mambo period in the 1950s.[46]

Hispanic Superstars

The influence of Mexican Americans on rock did not stop in the mid-1960s. Carlos Santana, born in a small Mexican town near Guadalajara, grew up in Tijuana. After moving to San Francisco at fourteen, he formed the band Santana, which played rock with a strong Afro-Cuban beat. In 1969 Santana played the Woodstock Music and Arts Fair. The group became an international sensation overnight after delivering high-energy songs such as "Black Magic Woman" and Tito Puente's "Oye Como Va."

Although Santana broke up after four albums, Carlos continues to create music. In 1999 he collaborated with some of the decade's biggest artists on the album *Supernatural*. The first single from the album, "Smooth," was a salsa-based rocker. The song "Corazón Espinado" was a collaboration with the Mexican rock band Maná. The album, with its irresistible Latin rhythms, went on to sell 15 million copies and earn Santana several Grammys.

Los Lobos is another Grammy-winning band from California. The group has sold millions of albums by blending rock and roll, folk, rhythm and blues, and traditional Mexican boleros and corridos. Los Lobos made several critically acclaimed albums in the early 1980s, but their breakthrough came in 1987 when they recorded songs

Carlos Santana and César Rosas of Los Lobos perform in New York City in 1991. Santana and Los Lobos are two of the biggest Mexican American rock acts.

for the sound track of the movie *La Bamba*, about the life and death of Ritchie Valens. The Los Lobos version of "La Bamba" became a number-one single. The following year, Los Lobos got back to their roots with the album *La Pistola y el Corazón*, which featured both original and classic norteño songs.

Los Lobos has flourished for decades as one of the world's premier Hispanic rock acts. In 2010, as the group was poised to enter its fourth decade in the music business, it released its fourteenth studio album, *Tin Can Trust*. The corrido-style lyrics, sung in English and Spanish, address modern problems such as poverty, survival in the city, and broken love affairs. The album, which was nominated for the Best Americana Grammy, features a mix of scruffy rock and roll, cumbia, and norteño styles.

Tex-Mex Border Music

The musical influences of Mexico are as strongly felt in Texas as they are in California. In Texas—which is called *Tejas* in Spanish—this led to the development of a unique style called Tex-Mex, or *Tejano* music.

Tex-Mex was initially created by bandleader Isidro Lopez in the mid-1950s when he added an accordion to his big band sound and began playing a combination of ranchera and corrido. In later years, Texas and Northern Mexican musicians added elements of norteño, rock, cumbia, American country, and blues to the style.

Traditionally, Tex-Mex groups consist of five- or six-member combos with drums, bass, guitar, horns, and a lead accordion cranking out a 2/4 polka beat. In the 1960s, the electric organ replaced the accordion in some Tex-Mex bands, which gave the sound a rock punch. The San Antonio band Sir Douglas Quintet, led by Doug Sahm, took the Tex-Mex rock sound to the top of the charts with "She's About a Mover" in 1965 and "Mendocino" in 1968. The group Sam the Sham and the Pharaohs was another popular Tex-Mex group of the '60s, with major hits including "Wooly Bully" (1965) and "Li'l Red Riding Hood" (1966).

The Queen of Tejano

In the 1980s, the Tex-Mex sound was updated with keyboards, synthesizers, electronic drums, and smooth pop production. With these changes, the style was more commonly referred to as Tejano music. In 1992 the popularity of Tejano grew quickly on both sides of the border after the Houston-based group La Mafia released the album *Estas Tocando Fuego*. Their record was the first Tejano CD to sell more than a million copies.

La Mafia's music appealed to bilingual music lovers, rockers, and even country music fans. The group toured and recorded extensively, paving the way for other Tejano artists such as Emilio Navaira and Jay Perez. While these acts sold millions of records, no Tejano singer was as popular as Selena Quintanilla, known by the stage name Selena.

Selena was a child prodigy who began her performing career in 1979, singing in her father's Mexican restaurant in Lake Jackson, Texas. She recorded her first songs the next year at the age of nine. During her adolescence, Selena played Tejano music in concert venues across the Southwest. Like Ritchie Valens, Selena did not speak Spanish, but learned to sing her songs phonetically.

In 1990 Selena released the album *Ven Conmigo* (*Come With Me*), on which every song was written by her brother, Abraham Quintanilla III. The album was the first recorded by a female Tejano singer to receive a gold record, with sales of more than five hundred thousand copies. In 1993 *Selena Live* won a Grammy Award for best Mexican American album. The following year, Selena's fame exploded after the release of her fifth studio album, *Amor Prohibido* (*Forbidden Love*). The album, which mixed Mexican cumbia and dance-pop music, quickly went gold. When Selena toured in support of the record, she sold out stadiums in the United States, Mexico, Guatemala, Puerto Rico, Ecuador, Chile, and elsewhere.

Tragedy struck, however, while Selena was at the height of her career. Like many recording artists, Selena had a fan club to keep followers informed about her upcoming records and tour dates. One of Selena's many admirers, Yolanda Saldívar, was president of the Selena Fan Club. In

Selena performs in Texas in 1994. She was killed at the height of her career, and her posthumous album was the first by a Latin singer to debut at number one in the United States.

early 1995, it was discovered that Saldívar was embezzling money from the singer. Selena agreed to meet Saldívar at a hotel on March 31, in order to retrieve paperwork from her. The women got into an argument over the embezzled funds, and Saldívar shot Selena once in the back. Selena died several hours later from blood loss. Her tragic death shocked her fans. Vigils and memorials in her honor were held throughout Mexico and the United States, and her funeral drew sixty thousand mourners.

Selena's posthumous album, *Dreaming of You*, debuted at number one on the *Billboard* music charts, making her the first Hispanic singer to accomplish this feat. On its first day, the record sold more than 175,000 copies, the most by any female singer at that time. In 1997 Jennifer Lopez played Selena in the movie of the same name, and the role helped make Lopez a major star.

A Universal Sound

Selena's music can still be heard on radio stations throughout the world, along with that of the latest Latino stars. In the twenty-first century, Mexican music has gone global with dozens of satellite, Internet, and cable radio stations dedicated to Latin rock, soul, rap, and hip-hop. Cable TV channels offer programming with cutting-edge sounds from Spanish-language rock artists including Maná, Kinky, Julieta Venegas, and Molotov. The Mexicana channel offers traditional styles with ranchera, banda, and mariachi artists such as Pepe Aguilar and Joan Sebastian. There are also stations dedicated to salsa, merengue, urban sounds, and Latin pop.

Music that has been forged among Amerindian, African, American, and European cultures in the past four centuries has become a universal sound. Without the influence of Latin musicians, many musical forms throughout the world might never have evolved. As it stands, wherever there are congas, claves, guitars, accordions, and trumpets playing joyous dance beats, the Latin sounds of the centuries remain alive.

NOTES

Introduction: A Global Beat

1. Quoted in Ed Morales. *The Latin Beat.* New York: Da Capo, 2003, p. xviii.
2. Morales. *The Latin Beat*, pp. xx–xxi.

Chapter 1: Roots Music

3. Laurence E. Schmeckebier. *Modern Mexican Art.* Minneapolis: University of Minnesota Press, 1939, p. 4.
4. Quoted in Robert Stevenson. *Music in Aztec and Inca Territory.* Berkeley: University of California Press, 1968, pp. 14–15.
5. Alba Herrera y Ogazon. *The Musical Art of Mexico.* Mexico City: Direccion General de las Bellas Artes, 1917, p. 9.
6. Richard Anderson. "Modern Mayan: The Indian Music of Chiapas, Mexico—Vol. 1." Smithsonian Folkways website, 2012. www.folkways.si.edu/modern-mayan-the-indian-music-of-chiapas-mexico-vol-1/american-indian-world/album/smithsonian.
7. Robert Stevenson. *The Music of Peru.* Washington, DC: Pan American Union, 1960, p. 39.

8. Stevenson. *The Music of Peru*, p. 14.
9. Dale A. Olsen. "An Ethnomusicological Survey of The Warao Indians of Venezuela." Florida State University, 2000. http://mailer.fsu.edu/~dolsen/advocacy/Warao/warao_indians_venezuela.htm.
10. John Storm Roberts. *Black Music of Two Worlds.* New York: Schirmer, 1998, p. 7.
11. Dale A. Olsen and Daniel E. Sheehy, eds. *The Garland Handbook of Latin American Music.* New York: Routledge, 2008, p. 86.
12. Roberts. *Black Music of Two Worlds*, p. xxiii.
13. Morales. *The Latin Beat*, p. xv.

Chapter 2: Caribbean Spice

14. Quoted in Maya Roy. *Cuban Music.* Princeton, NJ: Markus Wiener, 2002, p. 8.
15. Roy. *Cuban Music*, p. 8.
16. Roy. *Cuban Music*, p. 18.
17. Isabelle Leymarie. *Cuban Fire.* London: Continuum, 2002, p. 24.
18. Quoted in Morales. *The Latin Beat*, p. 7.
19. Quoted in Vernon W. Boggs. *Salsiology.* New York: Excelsior Music Publishing Company, 1992, p. 99.

20. Boggs. *Salsiology*, p. 84.
21. Morales. *The Latin Beat*, p. 84.
22. Wayne Marshall. "The Rise of Reggaeton." *Boston Phoenix*, January 19, 2006. http://thephoenix.com/Boston/Music/1595-rise-of-reggaeton.

Chapter 3: Brazilian Beats

23. Chris McGowan and Ricardo Pessanha. *Brazilian Sound*. New York: Billboard, 1991, p. 23.
24. Quoted in David Appleby. *The Music of Brazil*. Austin: University of Texas Press, 1983, p. 61.
25. McGowan and Pessanha. *Brazilian Sound*, pp. 29–30.
26. Quoted in McGowan and Pessanha. *Brazilian Sound*, p. 30.
27. Quoted in McGowan and Pessanha. *Brazilian Sound*, p. 38.
28. Quoted in Lisa Shaw. *A Social History of the Brazilian Samba*. Brookfield, VT: Ashgate, 1999, p. 7.
29. McGowan and Pessanha. *Brazilian Sound*, pp. 48–49.
30. Quoted in McGowan and Pessanha. *Brazilian Sound*, p. 68.
31. Christopher Dunn. *Brutality Garden*. Chapel Hill: University of North Carolina Press, 2001, p. 3.
32. Jan Field. "Boyz From Brazil—Brazilian Rap." The Free Library, 2012. www.thefreelibrary.com/Boyz+from+Brazil.-a018387596.
33. Alex Bellos. "Samba? That's so Last Year." *The Guardian*, March 11, 2004. www.guardian.co.uk/music/2004/mar/11/brazil.popandrock.
34. Quoted in Bruno Natal. "The Funk Phenomenon." XLR8R, January 5, 2005. www.xlr8r.com/features/2005/05/funk-phenomenon.

Chapter 4: Music of South America

35. Morales. *The Latin Beat*, p. 253.
36. Quoted in Roberts. *Black Music of Two Worlds*, p. 88.
37. Quoted in Camille Cusumano. *Tango: An Argentine Love Story*. Berkeley, CA: Seal, 2008, p. 82.
38. Quoted in Nicolas Slonimsky. *Music of Latin America*. New York: Da Capo, 1972, p. 61.
39. Quoted in Simon Broughton and Mark Ellingham, eds. *World Music, Volume 2: Latin and North America, Caribbean, India, Asia and Pacific*. London: Rough Guides, 2000, p. 363.
40. Quoted in Broughton and Ellingham. *World Music, Volume 2*, p. 366.

Chapter 5: Mexican Music in Two Nations

41. Dale A. Olsen and Daniel E. Sheehy. *The Garland Handbook of Latin American Music*. New York: Garland, 2000, p. 145.
42. Quoted in Broughton and Ellingham. *World Music, Volume 2*, pp. 466–467.
43. Quoted in Jacqueline Eyring Bixler and Laurietz Seda. *Trans/Acting: Latin American and Latino*

Performing Arts. Cranbury, NJ: Rosemont, 2009, p. 162.

44. Sam Quinones. "Tubas Become Horns of Plenty." *Los Angeles Times*, November 15, 2011. http://articles.latimes.com/2011/nov/15/local/la-me-tuba-20111115.

45. Morales. *The Latin Beat*, p. 290.
46. Morales. *The Latin Beat*, p. 288.

Afro-Cuban All Stars

A Toda Cuba Le Gusta, 1997

This album features a collection of old Cuban standards, mostly from the 1930s, '40s, and '50s. With a percussion-heavy, big band orchestra fronted by singing legends Ibrahim Ferrer and Manuel "Puntillita" Licea, the songs are perfect for mamboing the night away on a moonlit beach.

Pepe Aguilar

Por Mujeres Como Tu, 1998

Alcione

In the Bars of Life, 2000

On this live album, the Carnaval Queen turns her considerable talents to laid-back bossa nova, samba, and other classic styles. Backed by guitarist extraordinaire João Lyra, Alcione's singing invokes visions of smoky Rio nightclubs in the 1960s.

Seleção Essencial Grandes Sucessos, 2012

All Star Guajiros

Décima, Punto y Tonada, 2011

Babasónicos

Dopadromo, 1995

Jessico, 2010

Argentina's premier rockers take the listener on a musical journey through Texas twang, Mexican-western sound tracks, and Latin pop rock, presenting a digital version of the wild Old West.

Bajofondo

Mar Dulce, 2008

Banda el Recodo

La Mejor de Todas, 2011

Buena Vista Social Club

Buena Vista Social Club, 1997

This album reintroduced traditional Cuban *son* to a new generation, with stunning performances by veteran octogenarian musicians Rubén González, Ibrahim Ferrer, and Omara Portuondo. More than music, these sounds evoke magical spirits from a tropical paradise long lost to history.

Tego Calderon

The Underdog—El Subestimado, 2006

Calderon's breakthrough album blends hip-hop, freestyle rapping, salsa, and Jamaican dance hall into an adventurous reggaeton beat-a-thon.

Calle 13

Los de Atrás Vienen Conmigo, 2008

Entren Los Que Quieran, 2011

This album won a record-setting nine Latin Grammy Awards in 2011, and it is easy to see why. While the lyrics are more political than earlier Calle 13 offerings, the blend of musical styles on this record covers the world. Calle 13 touches on Jamaican ska, Dominican merengue, Hawaiian ukulele music, Bollywood from India, and folk elements from Peru, Colombia, and Brazil.

Cannibal & the Headhunters

Land of 1000 Dances, 2007

While the group may be remembered as a one-hit wonder for this album's title track, these East Los Angeles rockers put their unique Mexican American foot-stomping stamp on every song.

Beth Carvalho

Pérolas do Pagode, 1998

The Queen of Samba mixes traditional Brazilian sounds with African percussion on this tribute to the *pagôde* style.

Willie Colón

Cosa Nuestra, 1970

The Best of Willie Colón, 2012

Willie Colón and Rubén Blades

Siembra, 1978

Almost every song on this album was a hit single somewhere in Latin America. This pairing of two salsa legends sold more than 25 million copies and was at one time the best-selling salsa record in history. With lyrics that touch on Latin politics, American culture, love, and life in the barrio, the songs remain pointed and highly listenable more than three decades after their initial release.

Daddy Yankee

Barrio Fino, 2004

With the pop anthems "Gasolina" and "Lo Que Pasó, Pasó," this album introduced reggaeton to hip-hop fans from Vancouver to Vienna. With harmonious choruses, synth stings, and the ever-present dembow beat, it is easy to see why Daddy Yankee became the founding father of international reggaeton.

Gloria Estefan

Essential Gloria Estefan, 2006

Recorded with and without the Miami Sound Machine, the songs on this two-CD collection show Estefan at her Latin-tinged, pop-crossover best. Disc 1 is fast, consisting of salsa, disco, and other dance-floor hits. Disc 2 is the slow album, featuring Estefan's brokenhearted love tunes performed with Afro-Cuban rhythms, gospel-infused harmonies, and the occasional Peruvian panpipes.

Roberto Firpo

The History of Tango—The Complete Collection, Volume 1—Recordings 1937–1956, 2009

Juan Gabriel

15 Grandes Exitos de Juan Gabriel, 2004

Charly García

40 Obras Fundamentales, 2001

60 x 60, 2012

In celebration of his sixtieth birthday, the "Father of Latin Rock" released this set of three CDs and three DVDs recorded at a series of Buenos Aires concerts in 2001. The album features sixty of García's best songs taken from his solo career and from his groundbreaking bands Sui Generis and Serú Girán.

Carlos Gardel

Lo Mejor de lo Mejor De, 2001

Gilberto Gil

Barra 69, 1972

Although this live album has very poor sound quality, it is one of the only recordings available that presents Gil and Caetano Veloso sharing a stage at the height of their *tropicália* popularity.

Gilberto Gil and Milton Nascimento

Gil e Milton, 1976

João Gilberto

Getz/Gilberto, 1997

This digital reissue of the 1964 Grammy-winning album is smooth and super mellow. Listeners do not need to understand a word of Portuguese to love the sweet sounds on this disc, which popularized bossa nova among millions of fans the world over.

The Very Best of João Gilberto, 2011

Gotan Project

La Revancha del Tango, 2004

Live, 2008

The new tango sound of the Gotan Project mixes the traditional with the not so traditional. Their songs are informed at times as much by freestyle hip-hoppers and the jam band Phish as they are by tango godfather Carlos Gardel.

José Gutiérrez & Los Hermanos Ochoa

La Bamba: Sones Jarochos from Veracruz, 2003

This recording showcases the authentic *sones jarochos* sound of northern

Veracruz with a thirty-two-string harp playing at a joyous breakneck speed accompanied by the *jarana* and *requinto*.

Astrid Hadad

¡Oh! Diosas, 2007

Ivan y Sus Bam Band

Lo Grande de Ayer la Locura de Hoy, 1996

Victor Jara

The Greatest Hits, 2011

La Mafia

Estas Tocando Fuego, 1991

La Sonora Dinamita

La Sonora Dinamita—Super Exitos 1, 1994

Isidro Lopez

15 Original Hits, 2004

Los Fabulosos Cadillacs

20 Grandes Exitos, 1998

Hola/Chau, 2001

This pair of live farewell albums released in 2001 features the hits of Los Fabulosos Cadillacs played with an extra emotional edge. *Hola* reaches back to the band's early days and presents familiar tracks with a vital energy sure to please any rock fan. *Chau* consists of more "deep tracks" from the band's career with the audience singing along on every word.

Los Folkloristas

La Paguinita (Son Istmeño), 1981

Los Lobos

Tin Can Trust, 2010

Kiko: 20th Anniversary Edition, 2012

When this album was initially released in 1992, the combination of roots rock, Mexican folk, rockabilly, R&B, and Southwest country put Los Lobos on the map. Twenty years later, most critics contend *Kiko* is among the group's best records, which is saying a lot because Los Lobos has released many fantastic albums.

Los Paisanos del Sur

15 Zapateados de Pegue, 2012

Los Tigres del Norte

Corridos Prohibidos, 1989

MTV Unplugged: Los Tigres del Norte and Friends, 2011

More than forty years into Los Tigres del Norte's career as Mexico's hottest *norteño* group, this acoustic concert celebration of the band's greatest hits sounds fresh and relevant. The tracks feature a who's who of Latin stars, including Andrés Calamaro, Calle 13, Zack de la Rocha, Juanes, Paulina Rubio, and Diego Torres.

Los Yuras

Music from the Aymara and Quechua Andean Cultures, 2009

Machito

Machito & His Afro-Cubans, 1996

They don't call this bandleader Mucho Macho Machito for nothing. This collection of live performances from the late 1940s features a muscular collection of Afro-Cuban hot licks that can still scorch the speakers more than sixty years after the songs were recorded.

Maná

Drama y Luz, 2011

Mariachi Vargas de Tecalitlán

Sones de Jalisco, 2003

Sergio Mendes

Celebration: A Musical Journey, 2011

Merengue Latinos 100%

Merengue, 2008

Milton Nascimento

Club Da Esquina 1, 1995

Milton, 2000

This album, originally recorded in 1976, was the Brazilian superstar's debut in the United States. Driven by the saxo-phone of jazz great Wayne Shorter, the music is a magical mix of Brazilian beats, American soul, Beatlesque pop, and jazzy psychedelia.

Clara Nunes

Meus Momentos, 2003

Bis, 2006

Echun Okiry

Güiro for Elegguá: Music of Santería Live Ceremonial Afro-Cuban Music, 2002

Paquita la del Barrio

Resulto Vegetariano, 2010

Violeta Parra

Paroles et Musiques, 1997

Chano Pozo

The Very Best Of, 2009

Afro-Cuban percussionist and singer Chano Pozo is considered the godfather of Latin jazz. The thirty-eight songs on this compilation inspired trumpet legend Dizzy Gillespie to hire Pozo as a Latin drummer in his bebop jazz band.

Tito Puente

The Essential Tito Puente, 2005

The forty tracks on these two CDs mix instrumentals, Latin jazz, mambos, and the original recording of the classic

"Oye Como Va," which all demonstrate why Puente was known as El Rey ("The King").

Racionais MC's

Sobervivendo No Inferno, 2000

Ratones Paranoicos

Inyectado de Rocanrol, 2006

Is it the Rolling Stones or the Ratones? The Spanish lyrics are the giveaway, but the guitars and vocals could hardly be closer to Mick Jagger and Keith Richards. This is Argentine suburban rock at its finest.

Lucha Reyes

Serie Platino—20 Exitos, 1998

This album contains authentic Mexican music from the beginning of the recording era, featuring the unique voice and style of one of Mexico's best female singers—and one of the most influential. In major hits from her brief career, the passion and humor in Reyes's voice reach out from the distant past.

Lalo Rodríguez

Un Nuevo Despertar, 1988

Question Mark and the Mysterians

96 Tears, 2011

Santana

Santana, 1969

Supernatural, 1999

Selena

Live, 1993

Amor Prohibido, 1994

This album made Selena an international star and brought worldwide attention to Tejano music. With female-empowering lyrics covering unrequited love, cheating men, and her own family history, Selena mixes smooth 1990s dance-pop with Mexican cumbia dance rhythms. *Amor Prohibido* won awards, sold more than 2 million copies, and contains a Tejano sound that withstands the test of time.

Serú Girán

Peperina, 2007

Led by Argentine rock pioneer Charly García, Serú Girán's fourth and last album, recorded in 1982, presents progressive Latin rock equal to, if not better than, Yes, Genesis, and other English prog rockers.

Sir Douglas Quintet

Live from Austin, Texas, 2006

Mercedes Sosa

Corazón Libre, 2006

Cantora, 2009

This release, featuring two CDs and a DVD, was recorded in the last months of Sosa's life. With a voice critics called "a force of nature," Sosa brings together half a dozen Latin American styles in a celebration of social justice and song.

Sui Generis

20 Grandes Exitos, 2003

Tzotzollin

Mexihkateokwikameh—Sacred Songs of the Aztecs, 2004

Ritchie Valens

The Complete Ritchie Valens, 2010

Wilfrido "El Barbarazo" Vargas

Coleccion Diamante: Wilfrido Vargas, 2003

Various Artists

50 Vallenatos Inmortales, 2006

Afro-Dominican Music from San Cristobal, Dominican Republic, 1983

This record features examples of several different drumming styles from the African-influenced central-south region of the country.

Afro-Hispanic Music from Western Colombia and Ecuador, 1967

Amerindian Music of Chile: Aymara, Qaqashqar, Mapuche, 1975

Corridos #1's, 2010

El Ratón—Sones de Arpa Grande, 2004

The Mambo Kings (Soundtrack), 1992

This album consists of a collection of mambos, rumbas, boleros, and cha-cha-chas played by a stellar group of musicians, including Tito Puente, Celia Cruz, and Arturo Sandoval. For the film's soundtrack, the producers made every effort to accurately reflect the sounds of Cuban music of the 1950s, which helped the album garner several Academy Awards.

Mariachi Music of Mexico, 1954

Modern Mayan: The Indian Music of Chiapas, Mexico, 2004

Recorded in 1975, the music of the indigenous people of southern Mexico—made by subsistence farmers, shepherds, hunters, and artisans—expresses the ancient musical influences of the Mayans blended with both Aztec and Spanish sounds.

Planeta Samba, 2004

Red Hot + Rio 2, 2011

Second in a series of albums created to raise money for HIV/AIDS awareness and prevention, this edgy record is a tribute to the *tropicália* movement of the late 1960s. The thirty-three cuts feature collaborations of more than sixty international and Brazilian stars, including John Legend, Beck, Caetano Veloso, Seu Jorge, and Bebel Gilberto.

Rough Guide to Cuban Son, 2000

Sambando na MPB, 2009

Traditional Music of Peru, Vol. 1: Festivals of Cusco, 1995

The Traditional Sound of Cumbia, 2011

Packing a hefty load of fifty-five songs, this compilation features music from 1948 to 1979, each driven by the infectious cumbia dance beat. Disc 1 features country roots music, while Disc 2 draws from city sounds and best-selling stars like Anibal Velasquez. Collected by producer Will Holland over a five-year period from old 78 rpm records, these remastered songs sound so fresh they might have been recorded yesterday.

Caetano Veloso

The Best of Caetano Velose: Sem Lenco Sem Documento, 1990

Caetano Veloso and David Byrne

Live at Carnegie Hall, 2012

This acoustic pairing at Carnegie Hall brings together two musical giants and two national sounds. Veloso plays the airy Brazilian *tropicália* he invented, while Byrne contributes his quirky American Talking Heads hits that popularized new-wave music in the 1970s and 1980s.

Julieta Venegas

Otra Cosa, 2011

Paulinho da Viola

Eu Canto Samba, 1989

Acústico MTV, 2012

Carlos Vives

El Amor de Mi Tierra, 1997

On this recording, the tropipop blows like a fresh ocean breeze carrying sounds of cumbia, *vallenato*, and rock. The album includes "Fruta Fresca," the hip-shaking single that earned Vives several Latin Grammy nominations and charted at number one on *Billboard*'s Hot Latin Tracks.

Clasicos de la Provincia, 2000

GLOSSARY

Amerindian: Any of the indigenous cultures that have lived in the Americas since before the arrival of Europeans.

banda: Literally "band." A popular type of musical group featuring brass and percussion instruments that performs contemporary and traditional Mexican music.

bandoneón: A portable instrument similar to the concertina and the accordion that is popular in Argentina and Uruguay and is essential in tango ensembles.

bataque: A religious, circular dance ritual that was performed by African slaves in Brazil.

Carnaval: An annual festival that ends on Fat Tuesday and is followed by Lent, the forty-day period of abstinence before Easter.

corrido: A Mexican folk music style known for ballads that give voice to social struggles and political commentary.

cumbia: Music based on African drum rhythms that originated in Colombia's Atlantic coast; the dance is characterized by short, sliding steps.

décima: Literally "tenth." A traditional song style from Spain; its lyrics have ten lines of eight syllables each.

dembow: A popular rhythm sample based on DJ Shabba Ranks's single "Dem Bow" that became the basis for reggaeton.

ethnomusicologist: A person who studies the social and cultural effects of music and dance within a particular society.

favela: One of the extremely poor and crowded shanty towns, or slums, of Brazil, on the outskirts of urban areas. Dwellings are usually made from salvaged materials, and the neighborhoods lack basic services such as sewers and running water.

improvise: To invent words or musical phrases on the spot during a performance.

merengue: A music and dance style developed in the Dominican Republic with a very fast tempo, suggestive lyrics, and sensual movements.

multiplatinum: A term used to describe records that sell more than 2 million copies.

nueva canción: Literally "new song." A South American folk music movement associated with the progressive political and social ideals of the 1960s to 1980s.

polyrhythm: The simultaneous use of several different beats that creates complex rhythms commonly found in rock, Latin, jazz, and other styles of music.

ranchera: Literally "peasant" or "rancher." A Mexican folk music style with sentimental or nostalgic lyrics celebrating the natural world, lost love, and the simple life.

reggaeton: A contemporary pop music genre developed in the Caribbean that combines Jamaican rhythms and hip-hop.

rumba: A polyrhythmic Cuban musical style with strong percussive elements; the dance of the same name is known for intricate footwork and hip movements.

salsa: Literally "sauce." A dance music incorporating a variety of Latin styles developed by Puerto Ricans living in New York City in the mid-twentieth century; the name implies adding spice to the rhythm.

samba: Brazilian music based on African rhythms and strongly associated with Carnaval season. The dance is characterized by forward and backward steps, tilting, and rocking body movements.

sample: Short segments of prerecorded music recorded digitally and most often used in repetitive loops.

Santería: The descendants of West African slaves in Cuba developed this religious practice that combines traditional spiritual beliefs and deities with Roman Catholicism.

scale: Any sequence of ascending or descending musical notes. Traditional scales in Western music have seven notes, which make up an octave. Non-traditional scales can have four to eight notes per octave.

son: Literally "sound." The traditional, rural musical styles of a number of Spanish-speaking countries.

synthesizer: An electronic instrument, usually played with a keyboard, that produces unique complex sounds and mimics other instruments such as violins, drums, and horns.

tango: A music and dance style developed in Argentina and known for romantic lyrics and cheek-to-cheek dances.

tejano: Mexican border music that incorporates elements of ranchera and corrido developed in "Tejas" (Texas) in the mid-1950s.

tropicália: A Brazilian artistic movement concerned with social change and progressive ideals. The movement's music blended traditional Brazilian and African rhythms with rock and roll.

vallenato: Literally "from the valley." Traditional peasant music from Colombia's Caribbean region; the songs were used by farmers to spread news and gossip from town to town.

Yoruba: One of the largest ethnic groups of West Africa; many of the people of African descent in the Americas have Yoruba ancestry.

FOR MORE INFORMATION

Books

Mark Brill. *Music of Latin America and the Caribbean*. New York: Prentice Hall, 2010. This comprehensive book explores Latin music genres in their artistic as well as historical and cultural contexts. The two CDs that come with the book provide dozens of examples of important styles.

Cherese Cartlidge. *Celia Cruz*. New York: Chelsea House, 2010. This biography of the influential singer describes her music, escape from Communist Cuba, and immigration to the United States, where she was honored with a 1994 National Medal of Arts.

Patricia Greathouse. *Mariachi*. Salt Lake City: Gibbs Smith, 2009. This big, colorful book, filled with dozens of photographs, weaves together stories about life as a mariachi, biographies and interviews with mariachi superstars, and song lyrics. The book also includes a CD of mariachi favorites.

Tim McNeese. *Tito Puente*. New York: Chelsea House, 2008. This book covers the fascinating life story of the percussionist, arranger, and bandleader known as El Rey, the King of Mambo. It provides insight into the development of Puente's music, and explains how the percussion wizard influenced musicians around the globe.

Margaret Musmon. *Latin and Caribbean Dance*. New York: Chelsea House, 2010. Almost every style of Latin American music has its own dance style. This book highlights the development and influences behind dances indigenous to Cuba (the mambo and cha-cha-cha), the Dominican Republic (merengue and bachata), Argentina (tango), and Brazil (samba and capoeira).

Jeffrey Quilter. *The Civilization of the Incas*. New York: Rosen Group, 2012. This book explores the music, arts, and culture of Peru's original inhabitants including music and instrument used in ceremonies, celebration, and daily life.

Websites

Afropop Worldwide (www.afropop .org). Launched in 1988 as a National Public Radio weekly series, this site features a radio program, videos, and an online magazine dedicated to African sounds on nearly every continent. Listeners can enjoy music not only from African cultural centers such as Dakar, Senegal, and Johannesburg, South Africa, but also hear African influenced sounds played in the Americas from Chile to New York City.

Los Fabulosos Cadillacs (www.fabu losos-cadillacs.com). The official site of the internationally renowned Argentine rock band features music, pictures, video clips, and the band's latest news.

Smithsonian Folkways: Latin (www .folkways.si.edu/search/genre/latin). This site features sound clips from more than 170 albums of traditional Latin music from Central and South America and the Caribbean recorded since the 1950s. Some of the older albums include classic folk music from Argentina recorded in 1953 while more recent offerings include the Grammy-nominated *¡Cimarrón! Joropo Music from the Plains of Colombia* from 2011.

Sounds and Colours (www.sound sandcolours.com). This site extensively covers South American music, films, travel, and culture with news and reviews from Argentina, Bolivia, Brazil, Columbia, Peru, Venezuela, and elsewhere. This is one of the most well-informed sites on the Internet pertaining to top South American artists and their music.

World Cafe: Latin Roots (www.npr .org/series/145072962/world-cafe-latin-roots). This site offers radio shows previously broadcast on National Public Radio. The clips feature top artists exploring through words and music the Latin roots of various styles of music including mariachi, rumba, bossa nova, and reggaeton.

Films

Buena Vista Social Club, 1999
In 1995 guitarist Ry Cooder renewed widespread interest in *son* music when he brought together a group of legendary Cuban musicians (some more than ninety years old) and recorded a Grammy-winning CD in Havana. This fascinating, Oscar-nominated documentary by Wim Wenders captures the musicians' life stories, the making of the album, and the group's spectacular concerts in Amsterdam, The Netherlands, and at Carnegie Hall in New York City.

Calle 13: Sin Mapa, 2009
This documentary captures the Puerto Rican hip-hop and reggaeton act Calle 13 as they set off in 2006 to learn about the people and cultures their music has touched in Bolivia, Peru, and elsewhere.

Calle 54, 2000
This documentary made by and for Latin jazz fans was filmed in a New York City recording studio as a group of renowned musicians, including Gato Barbieri, Eliane Elias, and Tito Puente, jam individually and together.

La Bamba, 1999
This film tells the story of 1950s rock idol Ritchie Valens. It provides

not only a stunning depiction of the singer's Latin influence on U.S. pop music but also shows the obstacles Valens overcame to achieve success. The soundtrack by Los Lobos is a great feature of the film.

Los Lobos: Live at the Fillmore, 2004

The band Los Lobos celebrated more than three decades in the music business with a potent performance at the legendary Fillmore Theater in San Francisco, California. The show is captured in this concert film that features the group playing twenty-one songs in a variety of Latin styles, including Cuban jazz and even mariachi-influenced reggae.

Selena, 1997

Jennifer Lopez stars in this film in a Golden Globe-winning performance as Mexican American singer Selena Quintanilla. Selena's stunning success was brought to a tragic end with her murder at the age of twenty-three. The movie features Selena's great music and reveals details of her secret marriage to guitarist Chris Perez and of the conflicts she experienced with her father who was also her manager.

INDEX

PICTURE CREDITS

ABOUT THE AUTHOR

Stuart A. Kallen is the author of more than 250 nonfiction books for children and young adults. He has written extensively about science, the environment, music, history, and folklore from vampires to haunted houses. In addition, Mr. Kallen has written award-winning children's videos and television scripts. In his spare time, he is a singer/songwriter/guitarist in San Diego.